The Price of Patriotism

Indiana County, Pennsylvania and the Civil War

BY

W. WAYNE SMITH

PUBLISHED IN ASSOCIATION WITH THE HISTORICAL &
GENEALOGICAL SOCIETY OF INDIANA COUNTY

 BURD STREET PRESS

This Burd Street Press publication
was printed by
Beidel Printing House, Inc.
63 West Burd Street
Shippensburg, PA 17257-0152 USA

In respect for the scholarship contained herein, the acid-free paper used in this book meets the guidelines for permanence and durability of the Committee on Production Guidelines for Book Longevity of the Council on Library Resources.

For a complete list of available publications
please write
Burd Street Press
Division of White Mane Publishing Company, Inc.
P.O. Box 152
Shippensburg, PA 17257-0152 USA

Library of Congress Cataloging-in-Publication Data

Smith, W. Wayne, 1936–
    The price of patriotism : Indiana County, Pennsylvania, and the
Civil War / by W. Wayne Smith.
        p.   cm.
    "Published in association with the Historical & Genealogical
Society of Indiana County."
    Includes bibliographical references and index.
    ISBN 1-57249-099-3 (acid-free paper)
    1. Indiana County (Pa.)--History. 2. Pennsylvania--History--Civil
War, 1861–1865. I. Historical & Genealogical Society of Indiana
County (Indiana County, Pa.) II. Title.
F157.I3S64   1998   97-49400
974.8'89'03--dc21   CIP

TABLE OF CONTENTS

LIST OF ILLUSTRATIONS

PREFACE

Each year, as I tell my students, a veritable Niagara of Civil War books gushes off the printing presses. One would think the last word on the American Civil War had been written. Yet, historians find new lines of inquiries in every field and the American Civil War is no exception.

In recent years Civil War historians have explored the impact of the conflict on the homefront. Two studies in the esteemed New American Nation series synthesized with broad strokes the social and economic changes that the Union and the Confederacy incurred. Yet, as one historian has argued we need to get the "real war" into the books by examining local history and reconstructing "the stories of individual communities and their inhabitants." By exploring the local scene, he argues, we can more fully "come to grips with the diversity and reality of the war."[1]

Historians are undertaking such studies. In fact, the most insightful Civil War books these days are home front, not military, studies. While local in nature, these histories have utilized new methods and sources to explore the ordinary folk in the midst of war. In addition, the "new social historians" have applied their lines of inquiry to the American Civil War. By examining the community on the local level, the Civil War historian is revealing how that experience permeated American society. He is demonstrating that war has an impact beyond the battlefield. As a result of these microscopic studies, the historian is showing how the sinews of community were tested in critical times.[2]

This study of Indiana County, Pennsylvania fits directly in the genre of community studies and Civil War history. Though this area seemed far removed from the battlefield, this study demonstrates that the war had a measurable impact on the home front. Indiana County offered nothing unique in 1860. Its people, enterprises, and institutions were commonplace of the rural North. Using it as a representative area, we can begin to detect the wide swath that the Civil War cut across the American society. We can see the interaction between the boys in the field and the folks back home. We can gauge the impact of the war on the economy and society of the rural North. Above all, we can recognize that the American Civil War altered the lives of folks on the home front as well as the soldiers in the field for generations to come.

This study of Indiana County began as a teaching project. I decided to follow the course of a local community through the Civil War as a means of enhancing my teaching. Over the last five years, Indiana County in the mid-nineteenth century has become a research laboratory for undergraduate and graduate students. Many students conducted research, wrote papers, and discussed with me the Civil War, the "new social" history, and local history as a line of historical inquiry. It is only appropriate to acknowledge the contribution of the following to my thinking: Tom Arnold, Cynthia Caldwell, Rich Constanto, Doug Cubbison, Charles Day, Kim Gardner, Scott Harris, Dana Hegenstaller, Tom Hetrick, Valerie Jack, Craig Petrasic, Sonya Stewart, and Robert Waskowicz.

My colleague, Charles Cashdollar, has been a "sounding board" over the years and he graciously critiqued the entire manuscript. My running partner, George Walz, tolerantly listened to my Civil War stories as we racked up the miles. I also appreciate the assistance of Dave Kauffman, Phil Zorich, and the Indiana University of Pennsylvania (IUP) library staff; John Henry at IUP, who skillfully prepared the maps; Peg Ruddock and Melvin Newhouse at the Historical Society of Indiana County; Clarence Stephenson, Indiana County's premier historian; and, Richard Somers at the Military History Institute. The photographs came from the collections of the Military History Institute, Ron Palm, and Chuck Le Claire of County of Allegheny Division of Photography. Justin Tyme assisted with the proofreading and preparation of the index. I thank the IUP sabbatical committee for awarding me the time to complete this project, and the IUP Senate Research Committee for grants.

☆ CHAPTER 1 ☆

IN DEFENSE OF THE UNION

Impatiently the crowd milled around the terminal at Philadelphia Street awaiting the daily arrival of the train from Pittsburgh. Indiana Countians, on that late morning of April 15, 1861, lacked a telegraph link with the outside world. Consequently, they anxiously waited for the arrival of the Pittsburgh newspapers aboard the 12:10 p.m. train. As they waited, citizens speculated on whether or not the Southerners had forced the evacuation of Fort Sumter in Charleston harbor and what President Lincoln would do. Would the nation be pitched into war or could peace be maintained? Would the South achieve independence or would the Union prevail? As Indiana Countians argued these questions, they strained their necks and eyes for signs of the oncoming train. As regular as clockwork the clacking of the midday train sounded and the citizens saw the faraway locomotive appearing in the distance. They grew more restless as they anticipated the news which the Pittsburgh newspapers would reveal.

Unexpectedly the train slowed to a stop several hundred yards from the station. The baggage master, according to previous arrangements, threw off the bundle of newspapers to a young boy. The youth was twelve-year-old Henry Hall who had paid the baggage master dearly for the trick. Young Henry knew that his personal customers would be irate if he lost their reserved newspapers to the crowd. The newsboy grabbed the papers and sped for Sutton, Marshall & Stewart's general store where he could serve his regular customers and peddle the remaining papers to the crowd. As he had anticipated, the harried citizens soon arrived from the train station when they learned that Henry Hall had outfoxed them. Anxious for the news they surged into the storeroom, knocking over merchandise and bellowing out inquiries of the news from the South.[1] The headlines of the Pittsburgh newspapers boldly answered the questions—the Union had been attacked and President Lincoln had asked for volunteers to defend the Constitution.

Indiana County, like many small communities across America, was isolated in 1861 from the great throes besetting Washington, D.C. and Charleston, South Carolina. Landscaped in immense and thick forests of oak, maple, and northern pines, and located amidst the rolling hills on the western slopes of the Allegheny Mountain Range, Indiana County was principally a farming community. English and Scotch-Irish pioneers trickled into the area as part of the general settlement of Western Pennsylvania after the American Revolution. In 1803 the state legislature created the county and the federal census of 1810 reported that the county had 6,214 people. By 1860 its population of 33,735 was scattered among 3,389 farms and 3 small towns. The county's economy was highly localized in dairy and grain farming. Only 137 manufacturing establishments, principally flour and sawmills, dotted the county. The Pennsylvania Railroad linked Indiana County with its larger lines by constructing a branch at Torrance, just south of Blairsville in 1852, and then a spur from Blairsville to Indiana Borough in 1855. Indiana Borough, the county seat with a population of 1,329, was a small town of four streets (Oak, Water, Philadelphia, and Chestnut) lined with merchants, lawyers, blacksmiths, and tailors. Blairsville, a link on the Pennsylvania Railroad, was the second largest town with a population of 1,018. Saltsburg, having seen its "hey day" as a canal town, included 593 people.[2]

As with many northern rural counties Indiana County was decidedly supportive of the Republican Party. Republicans in Indiana County echoed the "free soil, free labor, free men" ideology of the national party. They believed that the future of American society depended on individual ownership of small farms where people could enjoy the fruits of their own labor and achieve a middle-class status. Labor, or hard work, to them was a virtue to be admired and the essence of a democratic people. When the Republicans talked of being "free," whether they referred to soil, labor, or men, they actually meant to use the term "unencumbered," a concept of no man being obligated to any other person. Only in this scheme of things, as Republicans envisioned it, could a democratic society be ensured for the future. Man had to have an opportunity to own land in order to move up the social ladder. A plantation economy such as that which existed in the South directly threatened the Republican ideology. The Southern plantation system was based on unfree people, denigrated hard work, and resulted in a society based on class.[3] In urging voters to turn out and cast a ballot for Abraham Lincoln in November 1860 the Republican voice in Indiana

Borough, the *Indiana Weekly Register,* broadcast the Republican Party doctrine of "Free Territory, Free Homes for Freemen, Economy and Reform."[4] Missing from this "free soil" doctrine was the militancy of abolitionism. Some Indiana Countians had preached fervently the abolitionist credo in the 1830s and the 1840s, and assisted some fugitive slaves to escape through the county. One countian, Albert Hazlett, had joined John Brown in the raid on Harper's Ferry in 1859. But the abolitionists exercised no influence on the county's Republican Party. Instead, former Whigs, like Judge Thomas White and his son, Harry, provided the leadership of the young Republican Party. William M. Stewart, a party stalwart in Indiana County, underscored the absence of abolitionism among Indiana County Republicans. He asserted that while the Republican Party "was opposed to the extension of Slavery into free territories it had no desire to interfere with that institution in the States in which it existed."[5] Indiana Countians attested to their devout adherence to Republican ideology by voting overwhelmingly for the Republican ticket in 1860. Lincoln, who won 56.7 percent of Pennsylvania's vote, carried 74 percent of Indiana County's vote in 1860 and won every district except Saltsburg and Cherrytree.[6] Republicans in Indiana County, the state, and the nation elected Abraham Lincoln of Illinois to be the first Republican occupant in the White House.

Southern extremists were unwilling to accept the results of the constitutional processes and Lincoln's election. They began to talk of withdrawing from the Union. South Carolina acted first by announcing on December 20, 1861, that it intended to secede from the Union. Secessionist talk spread throughout the entire South and other states quickly followed South Carolina's leadership.

The secessionist fever stunned Indiana Countians as it did the entire North. Southerners had threatened secession many times before but each time moderation had prevailed. Republicans believed that in 1861 the Southerners were bluffing again. President-elect Lincoln said that the "crisis would go down by itself." Indiana County Republicans initially agreed with Lincoln and the party leadership. The *Indiana Weekly Register,* the county's principal Republican newspaper, originally prophesied "that the tempest . . . will subside."[7] By Christmas, the reality of secession gripped the North. Newspapers talked of civil war, congressmen debated the possibilities of compromise, and lame duck President James Buchanan wrung his hands in fruitless anxiety.[8] Indiana County Republicans feared that the secession movement, thought originally to be a "mere gasconade of a few restive spirits," had attained fearful proportions.[9]

By mid-January the talk of military preparedness was sweeping through Indiana County as well as the rest of the nation. On a cold Saturday night, January 26, 1861, a few Republicans huddled around a coal stove in the Indiana County Court House to plot an aggressive response to the Southern secessionists. The group appointed a committee to solicit citizens who might be ready to answer any military call from the nation. The committee consisted of James R. Porter, the thirty-year-old prothonotary of Indiana County, his younger brothers, twenty-one-year-old Dan and twenty-three-year-old Robert, George Weamer, a twenty-one-year-old merchant in Indiana Borough, Joseph Hoffman, a twenty-three-year-old hotel clerk, and Hannibal K. Sloan, a twenty-one-year-old law student.[10] But other countians still clung to the hopes that compromise might cool the militant fervor and the attempt to raise a company of volunteers in Indiana, as James Porter would later describe it, "failed ignobly."[11]

When, on April 15, the news of the firing on Fort Sumter reached Henry Hall's customers, circumstances in Washington and throughout the nation had changed dramatically. Attempts at compromise had failed and rebels seemed intent on pursuing their independent course. As Indiana Countians mulled over the question of secession and the appropriate response, they, like many other Northerners, grappled with basic ideals undergirding the republic. They recognized that despite its great diversity and expansiveness the nation had one common thread binding it together—the commitment of its people to law and order. They understood that the challenge to the Constitution was more fundamental than the issues of South versus North, a plantation economy versus free-soil ideology, or states rights versus nationalism. At stake was the very concept of ordered society. If secession were permitted no future government—national, state, or local—was secure.[12] The secession of the South would establish a dangerous precedent. In the future, dissidents would threaten to withdraw from society over any cause. "A successful rebellion by a few States now will be followed by a new rebellion or secession a few years hence," predicted one newspaper.[13] Anarchy would replace constitutional government; factions would rule; military dictators would emerge; the United States, in the terms of the twentieth century, would become a "banana republic." Like President Washington in the Whiskey Rebellion, President Kennedy in the Montgomery Bus Boycott Crisis, and President Nixon in his resignation over the Watergate Scandal, Northerners in 1861 realized that our most valued concept, the commitment to law and order, must prevail. Indiana Countians expressed these thoughts in a variety of ways. The *Indiana Weekly Register* preached: "Government is necessary to preserve society and keep order in the community. No one, we presume, would desire to live without municipal government."[14] John Pollock, a farmer in Montgomery Township, said, "it is the duty of every man to use his money, his influence, and his life, if need be, to suppress this unnatural and accursed rebellion, and to defend our rights, our liberties, and free institutions against impending ruin, & anarchy."[15]

When the county courthouse bell tolled on the evening of April 16 for a meeting to consider a response to the crisis confronting the Union, the citizens in Indiana were ready to express their views, and they packed into the courthouse. Partisan differences disappeared for the moment. Democrats and Republicans, conservatives and liberals, joined together in this moment of crisis in a symbolic defense of America's nationhood. Hugh W. Wier, a prominent Democrat and lawyer in Indiana, presided at the meeting, and spoke for all when he announced that "it is the duty of every American citizen, no matter to what political party he may belong, to rally and defend the glorious 'Stars and Stripes.'—the banner of our common community." Other speakers joined Wier in denouncing the rebels' attack on Fort Sumter and urged that Indiana County pledge a "thousand men for the support of the government!" Harry White, the twenty-eight- year-old Republican lawyer, denounced the firing on Fort Sumter as violating the principles Americans had been taught from infancy. Joseph M. Thompson, a Democrat, confessed that initially his party allegiance had made him sympathetic to the South, but when the country was in danger he was willing to abandon all party prejudices for the sake of the Union. The citizens quickly adopted resolutions that upheld the "theory of man's capacity to govern himself," that party prejudices be put aside, and that a flag be flown atop the courthouse indicating the county's patriotic support of the Lincoln government.[16]

The following Monday, April 22, Indiana Borough was ablaze in red, white, and blue. Citizens hung flags in their windows and yards; every street flaunted its allegiance to the Union. Sutton, Marshall & Stewart raised the Star-Spangled Banner on the roof of their warehouse as a brass band piped patriotic tunes. At the courthouse, citizens gathered to attend a special flag-raising ceremony. Judge Thomas White presented the flag and the veterans of the War of 1812 raised it. But that spring afternoon dark clouds hovered on the horizon and before the ceremony ended a storm broke. Rain and lightning chased citizens to cover and high winds broke off the staff of the newly raised flag. Like the nation at large, Indiana Countians' devotion to the Union was being tested by the elements.[17]

More than symbolic efforts were occurring by this time. The regular army amounted to only 16,000 men and President Lincoln issued a call for volunteer troops from the states. Citizens across the northern tier of states responded like worker bees in a hive to the president's call. Individuals, who then would become the officers, signed up recruits for their companies. Throughout Indiana County volunteer companies quickly appeared. In Indiana Borough a meeting on April 18 resulted in Captain James R. Porter of the Indiana National Guard being designated as drill officer to solicit and drill volunteers. That night Indiana County registered its first soldiers to defend the Union when more than twelve young men eagerly volunteered for military service. These included J. S. Sutor, R. Harvey Fair, Daniel S. Porter, Hannibal K. Sloan, B. F. Laughlin, T. Moorhead Coleman, Archibald W. Stewart, T. R. Weaver, H. C. Howard, Frank F. Young, Theodore Henderson, and G. A. McLain. News came from Blairsville, Brush Valley, Chambersville, Kellysburg, Jacksonville, Marchand, Marion, and Shelocta of volunteers appearing. In Saltsburg, a company named the "Black Hornets" reported that its complement was full. Thoughtful patriots emerged using their entrepreneurial skills to assist the efforts of military preparedness. A special advertisement in the *Weekly Register* appeared on May 7 alerting readers to a book, entitled *Military Tactics*, available from the young Henry Hall. (After the war Henry Hall and his brother opened a book and stationery store in Indiana Borough.) Perhaps the volunteers of Indiana Borough should have listened more carefully to the young entrepreneur hawking his wares. When they met for their first drill, one remembered that "neither officers or men knew any more about the drill than the average Chinese did about the shorter catechism."[18] In the northern part of the county, John Pollock's volunteer company pranced in military formation around a farmer's field to the accompaniment of John McManus's fiddle. In one drill, Pollock, feeling a need to impress upon his young volunteers the seriousness of their duty, raised his sword above his head and vowed that it would never be captured.[19]

By mid-May some recruiters had failed to enlist the one hundred men necessary for a company. Consequently the eager soldiers decided to combine all units into a county-wide regiment. On Friday and Saturday, May 10 and 11, over 600 volunteers gathered in Indiana Borough. Nine units appeared in military formation, and their company names asserted an innocent bravado. Besides the Indiana Guards, there were the Indiana Fencibles, the Shelocta Invincibles, the Brush Valley Rifle Company, the Armagh Light Infantry, the Jacksonville Rifles, the Union Guards of Chambersville, the Cherry Tree Infantry, and the Black Hornets of Saltsburg. They elected Hugh Brady as regimental commander with James R. Porter as lieutenant colonel and William Cummins as the major.[20]

The patriotic fervor evidenced in Indiana County was matched throughout the Keystone State. Affirmations of military support and announcements of readiness from every county inundated the governor's office. Inquiries about uniforms, weapons, pay, and enlistment sites bogged down the mail going to Governor Andrew Curtin's desk. Letters from the volunteers in Indiana County requesting acceptance in Pennsylvania's army were merely drops in a great tide of military applications. Everyone was eager for an appointment, and a competitive atmosphere developed within the state and within counties between the various military companies. A Brookville applicant said he had seventy-seven "good strong hardy men from the pinewoods of Jefferson and Elk counties" in a company named, "the Curtin Guards," obviously to court the governor's ego. Indiana County's William Cummins advised the governor that his company, the Union Guards of Chambersville, was "the best company whose services were tendered from the county." Alexander Shoup advised the governor that he had a company prepared to march from Indiana County immediately. In this competitive atmosphere, eager soldiers were not above using political influence to gain the governor's attention. William M. Stewart, the prominent Republican in Indiana County, sponsored the Indiana Guard with a hasty note to the governor on April 19: "We have a company organized in this place ready to tender their service and have requested me to write to you & ascertain how they are to be furnished with arms." Harry White also addressed the governor "as one of the friends of your administration" and sought acceptance for his Brushvalley company. Harry was unaware that his father, former Judge Thomas White, did not want his son to go to war and used his political influence with Governor Curtin to get Harry's company deferred. Judge White reminded the governor that "I shall rely upon the conversation that we had in Harrisburg that his company will not be called up for sometime at least."[21]

Given the nature of the competition, Andrew J. Bolar, newly ordained Presbyterian minister in Armagh, was naive to think his company, "composed of students and Agriculturists mostly and consequently are entirely without military discipline," would gain any attention from the governor. A few weeks later Bolar's company had changed and was now "composed of young men mostly farmers and mechanicks who are anxious to do something in support of the government. . . ." In Blairsville, Captain James Nesbit feared that an apparent insult to the governor from an impatient and intoxicated recruit jeopardized the chances of that town's company being called. The recruit, W. H. Morgan, penned a most apologetic letter to Governor Curtin assuring him that "the company at large knew nothing of it. I was so much intoxicated that I did not know when sober what I had written. . . ."[22]

Notwithstanding the letters of endearment or insult, Governor Curtin simply could not cope with all the volunteers that poured into Harrisburg. He was obliged to turn away hundreds of companies from military duty. Among the disappointed were the Indiana County companies. James Porter decided to use all the political leverage he could muster from the county's leading politicians, and with their support traveled to Harrisburg to lobby personally with the governor. He carried a letter from E. P. Hildebrand, prominent Republican and the county's prothonotary, who warned: "Should this company disband, it will be impossible to re-organize it, or either of the other Company's [sic] now forming in the County. All depends upon the action of the Governor in regard to the National Guards. The disbanding of one Company, disbands all." That visit was followed by a petition from thirteen of Indiana Borough's most prominent politicians. They informed the governor that the Indiana Guards "have kept up their organization for the last three weeks at their own expense [and] many of them not in circumstances to bear it. Some of them are young mechanics that have been thrown out of employment. . . ." The petitioners advised the governor that Indiana County had "ten other companies ready to obey any call" but "our men are very much discouraged."[23]

The political pressure worked its magic for in a few weeks Curtin accepted Porter's Indiana Guard and Nesbit's Blairsville Washington Blues for state service. The two companies went to Pittsburgh where they boarded a train for encampment in Harrisburg. The train stopped at the Torrance Intersection on the Pennsylvania Railroad giving the soldiers a brief homecoming. The boys in the Indiana Guard hoped to see a crowd of folks from Indiana on the platform greeting them. But Indiana lacked a telegraph line and no one had been able to inform the town that their boys would be coming near the county. Consequently, only Blairsville folks were at the station to welcome the soldiers. Several of the young men from the Indiana Guard got off the train to meet Blairsville people and began to flirt with a particularly attractive young lady. As the train started to pull away from the station the soldiers reboarded, but in a hurried moment one of the Indiana soldiers turned to the young lady "and with the whole train load of young soldiers looking on threw his arms around her and kissed her then jumped on the moving train."[24]

The companies eventually reached Camp Wright near Harrisburg where they were given medical examinations and assigned to Pennsylvania regiments. Captain James Porter immediately met with disappointment. He suffered from a severe bout with rheumatism and had to resign from the army. Twenty-eight-year-old James

Nesbit had no difficulty with the medical examination and he remained captain of the Blairsville company. Nesbit was a particularly restless young man, who had just returned to Indiana County from California where he had gone in 1854 to pan for gold. The war would not dampen his restless spirit; his postwar life included years in Virginia and South Dakota as a farmer, before he finally settled down in 1889 in Indiana County. Nesbit's company became a unit in Colonel Richard White's regiment. Thirty-five-year-old Richard White was Judge Thomas White's eldest son. He had actively recruited some soldiers in Cambria County in April and gained an appointment as a regimental commander of the 55th Pennsylvania.[25]

The preparation for war intricately linked Indiana Countians together in a communal effort to defend the Union. The patriotic response to the crisis bonded countians together as no other cause or crusade had ever done. In mind and in heart Indiana Countians saw themselves linked to the Constitution, and to citizens in towns and cities across the nation. The subjects of "Union" and "Democracy" became the centerpieces of Sunday church services. Ministers in Indiana County devoted their time in the pulpit to sermons on the American Constitution and democracy. They exhorted the congregations to rally in defense of the Union. Women throughout Indiana County joined in community efforts to support the Constitution. They sewed havelocks for the soldiers and sent baskets of baked goods and fresh vegetables to the men in camp. Men from Indiana County opened up their personal and militia caches for the Union in mid-July and donated 131 muskets and 60 swords and two six-pound cannons to the Pennsylvania units. The martial atmosphere seduced young boys who played at soldier and fought mock battles with imaginary adversaries. One grandfather reported that his grandson practiced sword exercises because "he says when he goes to war he does not want to give a man many wounds as that would keep him in pain but he will cut his head off as then it will be all over." As volunteer units marched from their hometown to Indiana Borough to the train station, citizens lined the roads to cheer and honor the boys. When Captain Daniel S. Porter, now commander of the Indiana Guard, came home from camp to marry Sarah E. Clark the wedding became a celebration of youth, love, and commitment to family, community, and nation.[26]

As Indiana Countians mobilized their efforts to defend the Union, the battle of Bull Run on July 21, 1861, shattered illusions in the North that the rebellion would be short-lived. Two small, inexperienced armies clashed on that Sunday about 30 miles southwest of Washington, D.C. The Union army initiated the attack and nearly routed the Confederates. But rebel reinforcements from the

Shenandoah Valley blunted the Union offensive and turned the tide. By late afternoon Union soldiers and spectators from Washington were streaming to the capital city.

The first battle of the war demonstrated to the Lincoln administration that the rebellion would not be quickly thwarted. Citizens throughout the country now comprehended more realistically the will of the Confederates. That same mood was reflected by the *Indiana Weekly Register*. Admitting that the war against the rebellion might be longer than anticipated, the *Register*'s editor, August Row, warned that "the present conflict is going to be something more than a holiday pastime." Aware that talk of compromise with Jeff Davis's Richmond government had surfaced in nearby Elderton and that pro-Southern newspapers were circulating in the county, Row urged Indiana Countians to remain undaunted: "In these stormy times it becomes every true man to meet the crisis calmly but firmly. It is no partizan question that is to be decided. It is plainly a struggle to preserve the Government."[27]

The Bull Run defeat stirred other countians to positive action. In response to Governor Curtin's call for additional volunteers Indiana County became a beehive of recruiting activity. Richard White urgently wrote to brother Harry to assist with the recruiting: "Roll in, get me all the men you can. Send somebody out towards Cherry Tree." Captain Andrew J. Bolar, the young Presbyterian minister, gave up his pulpit in Armagh to lead his volunteers to war. His unit, accompanied by a stream of friends and a small band playing "The Girl I Left Behind," marched on July 23 to a railroad connection. William Cummins, a merchant in Chambersville, who had been captain of a private military club for several years, recruited his men to follow him to war. After a farewell banquet in Chambersville on August 27, they marched to an encampment at Kittanning in Armstrong County and later joined a regiment forming near Pittsburgh.[28]

On August 22, Captain Jacob Creps and his company of 110 men from the northern districts of the county boarded the train in Indiana Borough to join other units in Pittsburgh. This company was the union of two three-month units that John Pollock, a thirty-three-year-old farmer, had organized in East and North Mahoning, Montgomery, and Canoe townships, and Jacob Creps, twenty-five-year-old farmer and teacher, had recruited in Rayne, Green, and East Mahoning townships. When the call came for three-year enlistments in lieu of the three-month enlistments, many of the original volunteers withdrew their names. Creps and Pollock then combined the remaining enlistees, established Decker's Point and Marion Center as recruiting centers, and enlisted enough men to establish a company. Creps became the captain of the company and Pollock assumed second-in-command as first lieutenant. Creps and his men accepted a request from Oliver H. Rippey of Pittsburgh to join a regiment forming in the city. On August 21 the company gathered at Marion with "old gray-headed fathers and mothers, sisters and brothers, wives and sweethearts, with hearts wringing and eyes streaming bidding what was to very many a last farewell. . . ." The soldiers, their relatives, and their friends joined together in a mile-long caravan for the trip to the train station in Indiana. The procession marched through the community of Kintersburg where the citizens gave the soldiers a free dinner. Creps's men reached Indiana that evening. They boarded trains the next day, August 22, bound for Camp Curtin outside Harrisburg where they were officially mustered into the army and eventually became Company A of the 61st Pennsylvania Regiment.[29]

The recruiting enthusiasm extended into the autumn. On October 12 Captain Henry Altman, a fifty-eight-year-old carpenter from Indiana, and a company of sixty men from Indiana and Jefferson Counties left for military camps outside Pittsburgh. They intended to attach themselves to Colonel Amor A. McKnight's regiment forming in Pittsburgh. The volunteers included a small brass band of twenty-six musicians drawn from several counties, but headed by forty-three-year-old John C. Smith of Indiana County. The band proudly included twelve-year-old Jack McClain who went as the drummer. The *Indiana Weekly Register* boasted: "Although Jack is but a boy he is 'hard to beat' on a drum." Altman's volunteers became Company K in McKnight's 105th Pennsylvania. Altman soon found that army life was too rigorous for a fifty-eight-year-old and resigned in January.[30]

As the volunteers settled down in the camps, communications to and from the field bonded the soldiers with friends and relatives back home. Through the letters, many of which were reprinted in the local newspapers, Indiana Countians had a sense of the entire community being involved in this crusade to save the Union. From the 40th Pennsylvania a special correspondent, "Mitch," kept the folks back home fully informed of camp life. He regularly reported to the *Indiana Weekly Register* about the health of the Indiana Guards and the discipline in the army. Many soldiers were unaccustomed to handling weapons properly and accidental discharges were dangerously commonplace. One officer's horse, "Mitch" wrote, was accidentally shot in the neck. Other correspondents complained of the tedium of drill and the unappetizing army meal of bread, meat, coffee, and bean soup. On the other hand, Samuel Carbaugh, a twenty-one-year-old Brush Valley farm boy in Porter's company, wrote his brother, "We have very good bread and crackers and have fresh meat most of the time and plenty of coffee and tea it is as good as most of the farmers have about home." In a later letter, Carbaugh boasted that he was "fat and hearty as a buck . . . I weigh about 182 lbs this is my fighting weight." Another county soldier, stationed at Hilton Head, South Carolina, reported the balmy climate of the South. Comparing his Christmas Day swim to summertime frolics in Indiana County, he wrote that "I have been in Twolick creek in the month of June, when the water was colder than it was here on Christmas."[31]

Not satisfied with letters from the field, parents and friends personally checked on the soldiers in the army camps. Andrew Bolar's father and other Indiana Countians visited their friends and relatives during the winter. The bonds between home and field strengthened as folks back home tried to meet the material needs of the soldiers in the camps. In response to a call from the Quarter-master General of the State Militia, ladies of East Mahoning organized a committee to collect socks for the soldiers. They forwarded the supply to Sutton, Marshall & Stewart's warehouse in Indiana from where the items were sent to a state military store in Harrisburg. As Christmas approached, the women of Indiana County collected boxes and barrels of food for the soldiers in the camps. When the train left Indiana on Friday, December 20, its shipment included turkeys, hams, chickens, pheasants, cakes, and apples as holiday presents for the Indiana County soldiers in the Army of the Potomac.[32]

The onset of winter and the lack of military activity began to raise doubts about President Lincoln's war policy. Politicians, editors, and ordinary citizens grew increasingly critical of the administration and the generals. Lincoln, himself, lost his patience with General George B. McClellan, the commander of the Army of the Potomac, and ordered a spring offensive. The *Indiana Weekly Register* in December reflected the frustration surfacing throughout the nation. "Like thousands more, we are growing impatient at the standstill policy by which our army on the Potomac appears to be controlled", the editor lamented. "The country looks for action." Samuel Carbaugh had heard from his parents about "doubting Thomases" in Indiana County. Carbaugh responded: "Tell Billy Lewis to wait until we get a fight with the rebels before he concludes that the south will lick us . . . our Army is made up of brave men & not men that are afraid & dread the horrors of war at home."[33]

Additionally countians were growing concerned about the soldiers as reports of sickness and death in camps trickled back home. John Martin of Cherryhill died of measles and his body was shipped home to be buried in Penn Run. Typhoid fever was rampant in the army's winter quarters, and Indiana Countians could not escape it. Andrew Bolar and several members of his company contracted the disease and were hospitalized. Robert Craig of East Mahoning died of typhoid fever and others were dangerously ill. Joe Clingenberger, George Reed, and Daniel Shomber returned home on medical furloughs. Newly married Captain Daniel Porter was so ill he came home to allow his recent bride to nurse him back to health.[34]

Despite these demoralizing reports Indiana Countians remained steadfast in their loyalty to the Union and support of the boys in the field. The women of West Lebanon conducted a drive for blankets, socks, underwear, gloves, and bandages for the army. Volunteers continued to step forth and join companies throughout the winter. Recruits from East Mahoning, Canoe, Center, Armstrong, Indiana, and Saltsburg by early March had boosted the county's enlistment in the army to an estimated 800 men.[35]

The news of General Ulysses Grant's victories at Fort Henry and Fort Donelson in Tennessee in February 1862 boosted ebbing spirits in Indiana County and throughout the Union. Editors praised Grant's efforts as a mighty blow against the rebellion. The *New York Tribune* optimistically editorialized that "it now requires no very far-reaching prophet to predict the end of the struggle."[36] In Indiana County, the *Weekly Messenger* boasted that "one after another the strongholds of the rebellion fall into our hands . . . Victories are so frequent that they have almost failed to excite us."[37] Harry White wrote,"So flushed are we now with success that the people imagine the conflict is over. I do not think it is but believe the rebellion is much crippled."[38] R. Harvey Fair, one of the eager young volunteers in the Indiana Guard, was more optimistic: "If I mistake not the rebels are now beginning to feel sorter sick at the gizzard." Everyone wanted to hear the command "forward march." If the war commenced soon, he estimated that he might be engaged in duty "for at least six months more."[39]

The upcoming spring campaigns of 1862 would sorely try that optimism. Indiana Countians, at home and in the field, did not know that the blasts of war would test their commitment to the Union and to each other.

☆ CHAPTER 2 ☆

THE BOYS BECOME WARRIORS

Many years after the war, the men who went to war would remember that their youthful enthusiasm quickly waned once they had left friends and family. One remembered that on that fateful day, June 10, 1861, as he left with the Indiana Guard, he took one last look at a friend and "her form" that he was leaving, turned and went into a car, "sat down and cried, just like a whole lot more were doing."[1]

For most of the young men who went to war this was their passage into adulthood. As with young people in the twentieth century who go to college, obtain a job, or join the military, the enlistment in the Civil War represented a significant turn in their life's course. For the first time they were away from parents and old friends. Most had never been outside of Indiana County. Harrisburg and Washington, Virginia and Kentucky were only places they memorized from their geography books. They would soon cross rivers and creeks, like the Chickahominy, Rappahannock, and Antietam, which they had never read about in their daily lessons. Gaines Mill, South Mountain, Fredericksburg, and Gettysburg were unknown places which would become burnished on their memories. They left Indiana County, as naive young men, anticipating the glory of war; many would never return. Those that did were proud, but scarred; older, but wiser; fulfilled, but ready to get on with life. One of the Indiana County veterans remembered his naiveté many years later:[2]

> I shall never forget the morning when I lifted my hand under the folds of the starry flag and swore to defend it and the constitution. . . Then, it was the morning of our lives, nothing had aged, our wrinkles and scars were yet unrecorded on the fair scrolls of our hopes and ambitions . . . No wonder the flag laughed and only we were solemn, all ignorant of coming events.

As the historian tracks the paths these Indiana Countians trod during the Civil War, he wonders who these men were. From what kind of environment did they come? Why did they enlist so eagerly? What did they leave behind?

As we compare the differences between our world in the twentieth century and earlier times, we tend to focus on the improvements in our material life and the technological changes, the expansion of opportunities for women and ethnic groups, or the advancements in medicine and education. We sometimes overlook the "aging of our population." Here in the late twentieth century, the age group which is expanding the fastest includes those people who are over 65 years old. Grandmothers and grandfathers comprise a sizeable segment of our population; those under twenty-one years old are a declining portion of our population. One of the most striking features about Indiana County in 1860 was the youthfulness of its population. One might say that the county was comprised principally of teenagers. Nearly one-half, 46 percent, of the males were less than 15 years old. One-fourth of the male population was between the ages of 15 and 29. Nearly three-fourths of the males in Indiana County in 1860, then, were less than thirty years old. A veteran who remembered that the Creps-Pollock company from northern Indiana County included so many youngsters under twenty-one years old should not have been surprised.[3] The entire county was composed principally of "young people."*

The imagery of the Civil War tends to make the soldier appear as mature adults. In reality, we know that the armies are composed of very young men, and the survey of four Indiana companies bears strong evidence to support the more realistic assumption. Over one-third (36 percent) of the Indiana volunteers were less than twenty-one years old, and another one-third (38 percent) were in their twenties. Surprisingly, ten percent of the volunteers were over forty years old. Many of them quickly learned they could not keep pace with the rigors of army life and soon gained medical discharges.

Befitting their youthfulness, over two-thirds (69 percent) of the volunteers were unmarried. Most of them (52.6 percent) were listed on the census rolls as dependents. By being so young, very

---

* To better understand who the volunteers were I did a survey of four companies. Two of the companies represented the volunteers from the principal towns in Indiana County—Porter's Indiana Guard, and McIntire's volunteers from Blairsville. The other two companies were rural units—Bolar's recruits from the southern portions near Armagh, and the Creps-Pollock company from the northern districts of the county. By locating 81 percent of these soldiers in the 1860 manuscript census, I was able to gain a definitive picture of who these volunteers were.

few had had the opportunity to acquire any property; the vast majority (81.6 percent) owned no property. For the most part, they had not yet acquired occupational skills and were simply listed in the census as laborers or farm hands. Less than one-fifth of them were listed as skilled workers, and slightly more than one-tenth (12 percent) of them were either professionals, merchants, clerks, or students.

The homogeneous character of Indiana County is indicated by the 1860 census and the ethnic background of the 1861 volunteers. In 1860 only five percent of the county's population was foreign born. Indiana County clearly retained the character of its early English and Scotch-Irish settlers. Historians estimate that twenty-five percent of the Union army was foreign born, but for Indiana County, only two percent of the volunteers were foreign born.[4]

On a company to company comparison no real difference existed between the groups. The Creps-Pollock company from northern Indiana County tended to be an older group with more married men (44 percent) and owning more property (33.8 percent) than the rest of the soldiers. But, even in that company, the youthful nature of the volunteers bears true.[5]

By examining the character of the volunteers one can understand more clearly their motivations for entering the army in 1861. Undoubtedly, a sense of duty or patriotism played a large role. But the age factor unmasks them, too. Most of these men were unattached and had no property; or, in the parlance of the twentieth century, they had assumed no responsibilities. Consequently, they enjoyed a freedom to leave home, establish their identities, seek adventure, and return to Indiana County as men. Volunteering for them was the act of assertion of their manhood.

The Indiana volunteers in 1861 enlisted in many Pennsylvania regiments. Some joined in companies recruited in Indiana County. Others, eager to get to war, connected with companies that had formed in nearby counties. For example, some Indianans joined the Covode Cavalry in Westmoreland County and became part of the 4th Pennsylvania Cavalry. The companies that recruited principally in Indiana County and retained their local identity became units in seven different Pennsylvania regiments.

Porter and Bolar's enlistees became companies in the Reserve Volunteer Corps of the Commonwealth. Governor Curtin, fearful that Pennsylvania would lack sufficient men to defend the Commonwealth if Maryland joined the Confederacy, persuaded the legislature to create a special "reserve" division. It included thirteen regiments of infantry (30th-42nd Pennsylvania Regiments), one cavalry, and one artillery. The legislature allowed for this division to be enrolled into federal service and on July 22, 1861, the Pennsylvania Reserves mustered into the Union army. The 40th Pennsylvania had Indiana Countians scattered in Companies B, E, and I. Company B was the Indiana Guard commanded by Captain Dan Porter and Lieutenant Hannibal Sloan, a twenty-three-year-old, six-footer, who had been reading law under the tutelage of Hugh W. Wier. Company E comprised a group of enlistees from Blairsville. Nathenial Nesbit captained this company with D. R. Coder and Hugh Torrance as lieutenants. The 41st Pennsylvania included Company H, recruited from the Armagh area and led by the "fighting parson," Andrew Jackson Bolar. For a year Bolar served as both the captain and the chaplain for the regiment but resigned the chaplain's role because he "had promised the men before leaving home that I would remain and fight with them."[6]

The 55th Pennsylvania included Richard White's volunteers from Brush Valley and James Nesbit's enlistees from Blairsville. These soldiers were the first Indiana Countians to face fire in battle. Assigned with other troops on the South Carolina coast they guarded key ports at Port Royal and Hilton Head. In February 1862 the 55th was ordered to secure Edisto Island where it received its baptismal fire. White wrote home to his father that rebels used the cover of thick fog to attack the regiment which included Pennsylvanians, New Yorkers, and Massachusetts men. Nesbit's company from Indiana County was in the most advanced position and received the initial rebel attack. The company engaged in hand-to-hand combat with the rebels and the "Indiana boys [fought] like tigers." Several men were wounded and Billy Cunningham was killed.[7] Lieutenant John McElheney and 11 men were captured but most escaped by wading through swamps. McElheney remained a prisoner for a year. The regiment continued to serve on the South Carolina coast guarding Beaufort and Port Royal.[8]

The Blairsville Guards, captained by ex-postmaster William McIntire of Saltsburg, became Company B in the 56th Pennsylvania. Recruiting had been quite successful in Blairsville and many people believed with this company that the town had been drained of its manpower. It took over two months before sixty men had enrolled and the unit left Blairsville on October 24, 1861.[9]

Jacob Creps's and John Pollock's unit from northern Indiana County joined the 61st Pennsylvania Regiment organized by Colonel Oliver H. Rippey. The company suffered organizational embarrassment when it arrived at Camp Curtin outside Harrisburg. Officials wanted to assign the company to another regiment but Creps and his men felt an obligation to Colonel Rippey who was detained in Pittsburgh. They resisted the reassignment only to find that state officials repossessed all cooking equipment and insisted on retaking the state-issued uniforms. The men already had sent their civilian clothes home and now stood in the threat of being unclothed. Creps negotiated with the state officials to allow the company to retain its uniforms and receive rations. Rippey arrived shortly and the Indiana County volunteers joined his regiment as Company A.[10]

William Cummins' Chambersville boys and Michael Forbes' Cherry Tree recruits became companies in the 78th Pennsylvania Regiment. They left Pittsburgh on October 18, 1861, aboard steamboats headed for Louisville, Kentucky. There the 78th was attached to the Army of the Ohio to secure that border state against possible rebel raiders.[11]

John Stuchell, a farmer in Rayne township, recruited a few soldiers, and they joined the 103rd Regiment. The officers of this regiment had difficulty in raising the requisite number of troops to be an official regiment. The men were furloughed on the condition that they were to go home and bring back a volunteer. Stuchell went home and with James Morrow conducted a brisk campaign to find more recruits. They finally returned to camp with more soldiers and were officially mustered into service in January 1862.[12]

In the 105th Pennsylvania were numerous Indiana Countians including Company K which the fifty-eight-year-old carpenter from Indiana Borough, Henry Altman, had recruited. By January 1862, Altman knew that army life was too rigorous for a man his age and he resigned. Among the soldiers in Company K that Altman had recruited was Henry Hall's older brother, James. Captain Robert Kirk, a Irish-born, thirty-one-year-old redhead from Canoe township commanded Company F. The first lieutenant of Company D was J. P. R. Cummiskey, a twenty-four-year-old Catholic. His parents had urged their son to become a priest, but Cummiskey decided he preferred a law career. When war came he interrupted his studies to enlist in the 11th Pennsylvania and was elected first sergeant. At Colonel Amor McKnight's request he transferred to the 105th and was promoted to first lieutenant of Company D in February 1862.[13]

In the fall and winter of 1861–1862 the troopers were assigned to various regiments and they settled into the routine of camp life. Quickly soldiering lost much of its glamour. Unlike the twentieth-century military, the Civil War army had not fashioned the "boot camp" experience. Considerably more laxity existed in regard to discipline and order. Still, camp life rudely awakened the recruits to the reality of military duty. The young soldiers had to learn to march in time, face right and left, turn in columns and lines, and fire weapons in unison. Frequently, the military aspects caused less problems than the surrender of individuality, personal independence, and regular habits. One Indiana County unit, for example, found itself being called out for inspection on its first Sunday morning in camp. "Our boys, nearly all Presbyterians, United Presbyterians, and a few Methodists, declared they did not work on Sabbath at home," remembered one veteran, ". . . and they did not propose to break it now. . . ." Their appeal to the chaplain fell on deaf ears; he advised them that they were soldiers now and that they had to adhere to orders and discipline.[14]

Homesickness, disease, and filth quickly became other concerns of the soldier. Much to their surprise the volunteers quickly missed home and family. Nearly every letter home expressed a desire for more letters or lamented the lack of mail received. The first winter, 1861–1862, introduced the soldiers to diseases they would have avoided if they had stayed home. But the problem of bringing together thousands of men without careful sanitation triggered epidemics that swept through the camps. Initially, the childhood diseases such as measles, mumps, and smallpox plagued the army. The first wave was followed by regular camp diseases like dysentery, malaria, and diarrhea.[15] John Pollock, first lieutenant, Company A, 61st Pennsylvania, was among those hospitalized with a high fever. "Soldiers life is not an enviable one," he wrote to his wife, "money would not hire me to undergo the toils & privations of camp life, were not my country and honor at Stake, ..." He reported that twenty-two men in his company were so ill they could not report for duty.[16] Wesley Bell with the 78th Regiment in the West reported similar news of disease in the camps there: "There is 10 of our men halve the measles and 12 halve got cough fever or other diseases . . . it is awful to hear the moaning and lamenting of those that are dying."[17] The young men were also appalled by the lice and vermin. They had to adopt regular cleansing periods to rid themselves of the lice, or as they called it, "the blue and the gray."[18]

For young men who had never been away from home, the constant lament, yesterday and today, is that they miss "mom's cooking." The regular army meal of salt meat, beans, and biscuits added to the tedium and weariness of soldiering. The focus of many letters and memoirs was food. Receiving a package from home with dried fruits and cakes made that day's mail call a special treat. The soldiers frequently specified what food they wanted. As James Hall asked for envelopes and stamps from his brother, Henry, he added, "tell Ma to send a bottle of catsoup."[19] Conscious of the prices which soldiers had to pay in buying food from sutlers who went through the army, the young Hall demonstrated the entrepreneurial streak that seemed to run through the Hall brothers. Complaining that butter was selling for fifty cents per pound in Alexandria, Virginia, James wrote Henry that "if Butter is selling for 25 cents [in Indiana] . . . send 25 Pounds as soon as you can."[20]

John Uncapher, a twenty-five-year-old abolitionist who had fought in the civil wars in Kansas and voted to make Kansas a free state, returned to Indiana County and enlisted in Company E, 40th Pennsylvania. His diary reported that the soldiers freshened their food supplies with vegetables, hogs, and chickens from the Virginia secessionists. Forays to gather farm products and animals were common. At one time a Virginia woman put up the American flag to ward off foragers from her hog farm. But Uncapher noted that "it took more than stars and stripes to save a hog from hungry soldiers."[21]

Despite the many hours of drills and reviews, the soldiers had considerable time in which they had little to do. These periods of boredom and tedium weighed heavily on their patience and commitment to the war. Henry Hall's brother, James, complained about the inactivity and said that guard duty was the hardest work he was doing. Upon receiving a letter from Henry about life in Indiana, James wrote, "I gues that thery is more fitting in town than thery is hear you feles must have ben wild alot days"[22] John Park Barbor, another Indiana Countian, wrote disapprovingly of the manner in which the soldiers spent their time: "we lie and sit around waiting on the boats to come and writing letters. By some reason the soldier is loath to turn his attention to to books or reading. He is slothful and lazy." Pay day brought with it temptations that a young man may have avoided at home. As Barbor reported on one payday "Many spend nearly all their time in gambling. Some green hands spending all their money."[23]

On the other hand, camp life particularly if they were near Washington afforded the soldiers an opportunity to see the capital city. Barbor, like many other soldiers, took sight-seeing trips through the city and down the Potomac River.[24]

The army devoted these winter months of 1861–1862 to transforming young greenhorns into disciplined soldiers. Though flush with enthusiasm and eagerness, the recruits had to learn the intricate maneuvers a company or regiment took in battle. They learned these movements through constant drills and parades. As one historian has written, the drill training provides an understanding of the means by which large numbers of men move in battle. The drill also imparted a sense of "esprit de corps" to particular units like companies and regiments. The men gained a sense of confidence and identity, and began to see themselves becoming the soldier.[25] Yet, they had to be tested in battle. In the spring of 1862, the Union army for the most part was comprised still of volunteers who may have understood drill, but not yet battle. The Peninsula Campaign, May–June 1862, gave the soldiers in the eastern army their first real taste of war.

General George B. McClellan, commander of the Army of the Potomac, the principal Union army in the East, designed a plan whereby his army would launch an invasion on the Virginia Peninsula formed by the James and York Rivers, and the Chesapeake Bay. From there, McClellan determined that his army would drive inland and capture Richmond, the Confederate capital. In March and April 1862 stages of his army moved down the Chesapeake Bay to Fortress Monroe, a Union outpost, on the peninsula.

Upon his arrival on the Virginia Peninsula with the Army of the Potomac, Lieutenant John Pollock, the farmer from Montgomery township, learned that his wife had died. Aware that Mrs. Pollock had been seriously ill, Lieutenant Pollock applied for a furlough to attend to family business and their children. But the Army of the Potomac's movement south superseded the personal concerns of one individual and Pollock's pleas for temporary leave went unattended. Now with the army engaged in rebel territory, grief-stricken Pollock cried that "I am obliged to Stand at my post and bear my burden of grief. . . ." He asked his father to attend to his property and to see that the grain was not stolen. Within a month Pollock's grief was compounded by the news that his four children were suffering with the dreaded disease, whooping cough. He appealed to his sister to attend to his children and sent $5 home to care for them. While, indeed, he mourned silently over the loss of his wife, Pollock reported that the spirits of the troops were quite high and that they hoped to take Richmond before the end of the week.[26] Pollock and the Indiana soldiers did not have long to wait; on May 31, they found themselves engaged in the battle of Fair Oaks.

The Army of the Potomac, nearly 100,000 strong, easily overran Confederate defenses at Yorktown and Williamsburg in May and by the end of the month bivouacked within seven miles of the rebel capital. Yankee soldiers heard the churchbells ring and saw the tops of some of the taller buildings in the city. But McClellan had situated his troops in a poor configuration, and that was to be the basis of defeat. Violating all military sense he stationed his army so that the Chickahominy River, now swollen from heavy spring rains, intersected his lines. The two segments of the army were connected only by temporary bridges which the engineers had quickly constructed. Exposed on the left wing of the Union army was Major General Erasmus D. Keyes's IV Corps. It was south of the Chickahominy, holding a position on the Richmond and York Railroad at Fair Oaks Station, about six miles outside Richmond. Among Keyes's troopers were Indiana Countians in the 61st Pennsylvania. It was this corps that became a Confederate target.

Intending to overrun the Union's isolated IV Corps, the Confederate commander, Joe Johnston, launched an attack on May 31. Fortunately for the Union army, Johnston's plans went awry. Longstreet's division took the wrong road and delayed the attack until midday. Rather than a coordinated offensive, the battle became disjointed, or as one historian wrote, "phenomenally mismanaged."[27] Despite these inauspicious conditions the Confederate offensive focused on the earthworks along the line of the IV Corps. In fierce fighting the massed Confederate attack repeatedly pummelled the Union line. The Confederates pushed through the earthworks and threatened a major breakthrough of the entire IV Corps's line.

The 61st Pennsylvania waited in line as the battle began. About noon the divisional commander, General Couch, ordered the 61st up to the Richmond Road to reinforce the Union line. As the unit moved into the deep forests on the battle line Couch explained to Colonel Rippey of the 61st Pennsylvania, "This is a forlorn hope. Hold the enemy back at all hazards." The regiment, including Jacob Creps's Indiana County boys as Company A, was armed with obsolete smoothbore Mexican War muskets. Advancing through the thick forests in quick time the 61st came upon a rebel column that was heading to meet them. Rippey quickly ordered his men to file right to establish a line to confront the rebel advancing column. The Confederates performed a similar maneuver and within minutes hostile soldiers faced each other only twenty yards apart. The Confederates opened fire first. Rippey, giving the commands, "Ready, aim, fire," was instantly killed. Other officers quickly fell. As Union and rebel weapons cracked at one another, the Union position sagged. Confederates poured through a gap and turned on the flank of other Union regiments. The 61st Pennsylvania found itself outflanked and for over two hours engaged in a firefight with charging rebels. Exhausting their supply of ammunition the Pennsylvanians pulled back only to encounter rebels on their rear. A fierce hand-to-hand life-and-death struggle ensued as the soldiers of the 61st tried to cut their way out of the enveloping Confederate mass. Creps and Pollock slashed at the rebels with their swords and revolvers; the enlisted men swung their empty guns as clubs to bash heads. Pollock found himself surrounded by rebels and they hollered at him to surrender the sword which he vowed never to give up. Bullets ripped into his body and he fell to the ground gripping his sword and firing his revolver. Most of the Pennsylvanians cut their way through the charging rebel lines and escaped back to Union lines. They were able to drag some of the wounded with them, including Pollock.[28]

The III Corps moved forward to assist the retreating Union soldiers. Included in these reinforcements was the 105th Pennsylvania organized by Captain Amor A. McKnight with recruits from Indiana and Jefferson counties. About 4:00 p.m. the soldiers of the 105th entered the fight. They advanced to the IV Corps's earthworks where they found the rebels waiting for them. Under heavy artillery and rifle fire from the emplaced rebels the 105th charged. They recaptured the earthworks and held their position until 7:15 p.m. when re-enforced rebels counterattacked. Low on ammunition and his ranks depleted, McKnight decided to take advantage of the onset of evening darkness and ordered a retreat. The 105th slipped into the fallen timber and swamps, and escaped undiscovered. The 105th's soldiers clearly understood their precarious position. "We only held our ground that we occupied," James Hall reported, "and if they had of got one started they would of run us back to whair we started from and maybe farther."[29]

The battle of Fair Oaks ended in a stalemate with both sides suffering terrible losses. Especially hard hit was the 61st Pennsylvania which lost 263 men killed, wounded, or missing. The regiment lost 55.4 percent of the men engaged; no other Federal unit lost as many men in this battle as did the 61st Pennsylvania.[30] Brigade commander, General John J. Abercrombie, reported that "no field officer of the Sixty-first Pennsylvania is left to make out the report of that regiment. . . ."[31] The regimental commander Oliver Rippey was killed as were other field officers. Captain Creps of the Indiana County company suffered a slight wound but retained command; the Second Lieutenant George W. Brady's wounds were so severe he had to resign from the army. Also among the badly wounded was Lieutenant Pollock, recent widower and father of four children. He died two weeks later on June 13 in a hospital in Portsmouth, Virginia.[32]

In this day of terrible losses for Pennsylvania troops, the 105th bled badly, too. It lost over 161 men of which 41 were killed in action. Among the men lost was Lieutenant Cummiskey, the young Catholic, whose parents had dreamed of a priesthood for their son. He "had his head blown off by a cannon ball while gallantly leading his men forward to repulse a charge of the enemy."[33]

After the frightful engagement at Fair Oaks, the two armies settled down for a month's rest. The Army of the Potomac remained around the swamps of the Chickahominy River. The army's extreme right wing, the V Corps, became the target of the new Confederate commander, Robert E. Lee. On June 26 the lines reopened fire as the first of the Seven Days' Battle began. The Union line came under attack at Mechanicsville, and was driven back to Gaines Mill. The next day, June 27, Lee's army charged again and the Union forces found themselves under a horrific attack. The Union center collapsed under the Confederate attack and the army retreated again. In this engagement segments of the Pennsylvania Reserve units were captured. John Uncapher, Company E, 40th Pennsylvania noted that gunsmoke enveloped the lines "and our officers were unable to see to the right or left and the line gave way on both our flanks and we became entirely surrounded by the enemy."[34] After a few weeks in Libby Prison in Richmond the captured Pennsylvanians were exchanged and rejoined the Union army.

Meanwhile McClellan, unnerved by Lee's powerful assault, feared that he would lose the entire army. For the next several days he pulled his army back to a more secure position on the James River. As McClellan's army retreated, the Confederate army mounted dogged attacks at Savage Station, Frasyer's Farm (Charles City Crossroads), and Malvern Hill.

The Indiana Guard in Company B, 40th Pennsylvania happened to be detached from the mother regiment at the battle of Gaines Mill. The Indiana Countians were behind the lines making axe handles. They missed the battle and escaped being captured. But, seeing the army retreating and in disarray, Captain Porter gathered together 106 men, organized two companies, one under command of Lieutenant Hannibal K. Sloan, and attached themselves to the 38th Pennyslvania. Later in the day they encountered some fire and lost their first two men in battle, R. Harvey Fair and Moses B. Charles. Fair had been one of the young men who leaped over the railing in the Indiana Court House to volunteer in April 1861. Now, one year later, he had been captured, had his leg amputated by Confederate surgeons, had become delirious and died.[35]

As the Union army retreated through the swamps and dense forests of Virginia towards the James River, the battered Pennsylvania Reserve defended a strategic intersection at New Market, the Charles City Crossroads. On June 30 the Pennsylvanians engaged a relentless Confederate force for control of the crossroads. About 3 o'clock in the afternoon the Pennsylvanians saw a powerful, screaming tide of Confederates running to overtake their position.

For Porter and Sloan's men this was their first direct engagement, but it was as savage as any confrontation that anyone had encountered. The Indiana troops formed a line around a six-gun battery where they met a ferocious attack from Alabama regiments. The Pennsylvania troops and batteries drove back a brigade of rebels, only to meet a second, and then a third. The Pennsylvanians could not stem the Confederate tide and both lines were pitched into one of the rare bayonet fights of the war. The men under Captain Porter, determined to avenge the capture of their comrades, fought in the hand-to-hand conflict. Charles Shambaugh spotted a color bearer at the front of the rebel line, dashed out, knocked the rebel down, grabbed the colors, and ran back into Company B's midst, stuttering "I go-go-got the d-d-d——thing." Sergeant Henderson Howard found himself under attack from four rebels. He shot one man, bayonetted two, and chased the fourth away. Curly headed James Jethro audaciously chased some rebels into the woods that was full of Longstreet's men. He never returned. Porter reported that "every inch was contested. My boys only left the field when night put an end to the fray." At day's end Company B, the Indiana Guard, displayed a trophy—a battle flag which Corporal Charles Shambaugh had captured. Yet, it was a costly engagement; 56 men of the company's 106 complement were wounded, missing, or killed. For their bravery in this engagement Sergeant Howard and Corporal Shambaugh received the Congressional Medal of Honor.[36]

For the Union army the battle at the Charles City Crossroads was another bloody loss. But the engagement gave McClellan time to pull his entire army together at the James River where they met Lee's final attack the next day, July 1, at Malvern Hill.

The ranks of the Pennsylvania Reserves were too decimated for them to fight on the forward lines at Malvern Hill. Other Indiana County soldiers were deeply engaged in this last battle of McClellan's Peninsula Campaign. The 61st and 105th Regiments came into line to defend the Union's artillery position against Lee's advancing columns. Creps's men in the 61st Pennsylvania supported a battery on the left of the Union line and drove off repeated rebel attacks. The 105th fought in intense fire for over four hours as it defended the Union line behind a rail fence. "We was not there very long till we commenced firing. We fired over one hundred rounds of cartridge apiece," wrote James Hall, before they were relieved. The Confederates came within twenty-five yards of the 105th's position before rifle and artillery fire drove them back.[37]

Lee's assaults not could dislodge or overwhelm the Union army at Malvern Hill. Driving forward into the belching mouths of the Union cannon proved to be too costly for the Confederates. Lee's army had to retire from the field and allow the Union army to escape from the Virginia Peninsula. For the Confederates the campaign, though costly, was successful. They had defended Richmond and driven the Union army from the field.

The campaigning moved into northern Virginia a few weeks later as Lee attempted to defeat a newly organized Union army outside

Washington, D.C., at Manassas Junction, or Bull Run. This second battle of Bull Run, August 29–30, 1862, occurred when a daring Confederate force under Stonewall Jackson lured General John Pope's army into battle. Expecting to overcome a small Confederate force, the Union army soon found itself outflanked by reinforcements under General James Longstreet.

The Indiana County soldiers found themselves in the midst of the battle again. The Pennsylvania Reserve, the 56th Pennsylvania, and the 105th Pennsylvania held positions in the center of the Union line which bore the brunt of the battle. G. Adams McClain, of Company B, reported afterward of the confusion in the Union lines. On August 29, the company rushed into a masked battery and were taken by surprise. The Confederate artillery raked their lines with grape, canister, and shell fire. The next day, he wrote, "we were ordered to fight against the fiercest fire imaginable . . . we were outflanked and had to fall back to save the regiment from being surrounded. . . ."[38] One veteran later remembered the confusion in the command of the army and the constant marching which exhausted the soldiers before the battle. "It was evident in the minds of every private in the ranks that some one had blundered and no one wished to shoulder the blame."[39] General Samuel Jackson of the 40th Pennsylvania confided to his diary that his regiment had only one hundred fighting men available after the battle. "We are completely worn out," he wrote.[40] An Indiana County volunteer, Samuel William Campbell, who had just arrived in Washington observed the disarray and demoralization that came with the defeat at Second Bull Run. "Our Army is a good deal scattered," he reported. "The streets are full of them passing and repassing, hunting their company and regiments." Then he noted that some of his friends from Indiana County suffered in the battle:[41]

> Samuel Cunningham was wounded Aug. 30th, one bullet put clean through his stomach, his arm broken, a bullet put through his leg and he walked two miles off the battle field and he has the vitals coming out of his stomach and no more is heard of him. . . John M. Mack is wounded in the shoulder. Wm. Mack has one of his legs shot off, and Hugh Orr is wounded in the shoulder.

After his successful victory at the battle of Second Bull Run, General Robert E. Lee took the Army of Northern Virginia into the north. Hoping either to convince secessionists in Maryland to join the Confederacy, to encourage the peace movement in the upcoming autumn elections, or to demonstrate rebel strength to gain England's and France's recognition of the Confederacy, Lee's campaign took on momentous significance. On Thursday, September 4, 1862, Lee's

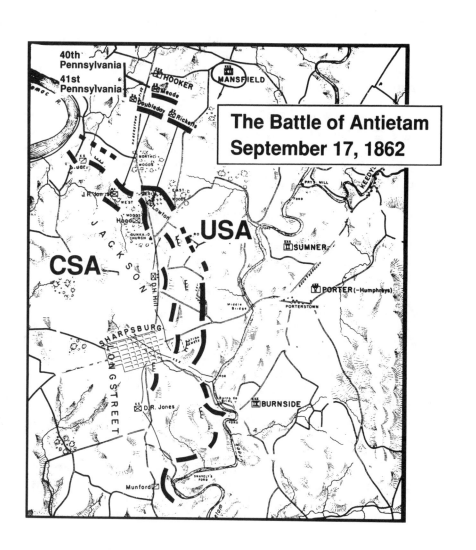

The Battle of Antietam
September 17, 1862

advance units crossed the Potomac and for the first time the Confederate army invaded the Union.

Ten days later, George B. McClellan and the Army of the Potomac overtook segments of Lee's army in the mountain passes between Frederick and Hagerstown, Maryland. As Lee's army attempted to regroup itself, trailing units defended the passes known as Turner's Gap and Crampton's Gap on South Mountain. On Sunday, September 14, rebel and Union soldiers contested one another all day in a desperate battle for control of the passes. The Pennsylvania Reserve, including the Indiana County boys, attacked the Confederates who occupied the high ground overlooking Turner's Gap. The Pennsylvanians went tree to tree, rock to rock, step by step up the mountain against raining bullet fire from the Confederates. By sunset the Union soldiers reached the summit and controlled the passes running through South Mountain. After the battle, Captain Dan Porter went among the men complimenting them for the hearty fight they had shown and told them that he believed the battle for South Mountain was the fiercest engagement his soldiers had seen. The losses were heavy and General Jackson noted that the 40th Pennsylvania was "nearly annihilated." From Indiana County, the casualties included Company E's Captain Nathaniel Nesbit and Color Sergeant James L. Hazlett, who were mortally wounded.[42]

Finally, on September 17, the Army of the Potomac pinned down Lee's army outside Sharpsburg, Maryland, a small country hamlet near Antietam Creek's flow into the Potomac River. The Union troops had the rebels on the run and McClellan anticipated a knockout blow. He planned for simultaneous assaults from Hooker's I Corps, Mansfield's XII Corps, and Burnside's IX Corps against the entrenched Confederates. But delays on the field turned the battle of Antietam into a combination of disjointed attacks.

Sixty units, including artillery and infantry, represented Pennsylvania in the battle of Antietam. Among these troopers were several companies from Indiana County who were in Hooker's I Corps on the extreme right wing of the Union army. The Indiana Guard and Blairsville units were in the Pennsylvania Reserve under General George Meade, and Doubleday's 56th Regiment included McIntire's Blairsville Company. It was Hooker's Corps, 8,600 men strong, that opened the battle at six o'clock in the morning. The troops of this corps advanced in column formation through a cornfield towards the rebel line in the West Woods and around Dunker Church. Encountering murderous fire from rebel artillery and rifles, the I Corps sustained its drive only by pouring more soldiers into the assault. Porter's Indiana Company in the 40th Pennsylvania and Bolar's company in the 41st Pennsylvania were among those soldiers advancing through the cornfield under heavy fire.

Bolar, reporting for his regiment, described the assault:[43]

. . . coming into an open field and to the top of a hill where we deployed into line of battle in front of a corn-field occupied by the enemy. Here we replied to their fire, which began to take effect on our ranks, and advanced firing to a fence, behind which we took position, keeping up constant musketry . . . We then crossed the fence, advanced to the top of the hill in full view of the enemy under a terrible fire, which killed and wounded nearly one-half of the command . . .

They lost 64 men killed or wounded in this charge. Among those was Tom S. Moore, in Company B, who had hurriedly left a hospital to rejoin his company. At one point in the charge Moore took aim on a rebel color bearer and fired. As the rebel flag fell, Moore jumped up with excitement. Instantly a minie ball pierced his chest. He died the next morning.[44] A see-saw battle in the cornfield and around Dunker Church ensued throughout the morning between Hooker's I Corps and the Confederates before Mansfield's XII Corps took up the attack. Exhausted and decimated the I Corps had to retire from battle. It had lost nearly one-third of the men engaged. The battle continued throughout the day along the line, finally ending at sunset in another bloody stalemate. McClellan lost twenty-five percent of the men he had put into battle, Lee, thirty-one percent. The combined total of losses was 22,719, making September 17, 1862, the bloodiest day of the war.[45]

Indiana Countians counted in the grim statistics of Antietam. Only Samuel Ray, Henry Prothero, and John Smith in Company B escaped the battle without a wound. Captain Dan S. Porter, Company B, offered a somber perspective: "It was a terrible battle and the slaughter was awful. It was sickening to pass over the bloody field . . . ."[46]

After the battle of Antietam Lee retreated southward with his badly mauled army. President Lincoln, exasperated with McClellan's indecisiveness, appointed General Ambrose Burnside as the new commander of the Army of the Potomac. Burnside plotted a new battle plan and marched his army due south towards Richmond. At Fredericksburg, Virginia, a small town on the Rappahannock River in December 1862, Burnside found Lee's army blocking the way. Rather than maneuvering around the Confederate position Burnside decided to attack it. He saw that Lee's soldiers occupied Marye's Heights and Prospect Hill which lay behind Fredericksburg, but Burnside believed simultaneous assaults could dislodge the rebels. On December 13, 1862, Burnside ordered two major assaults

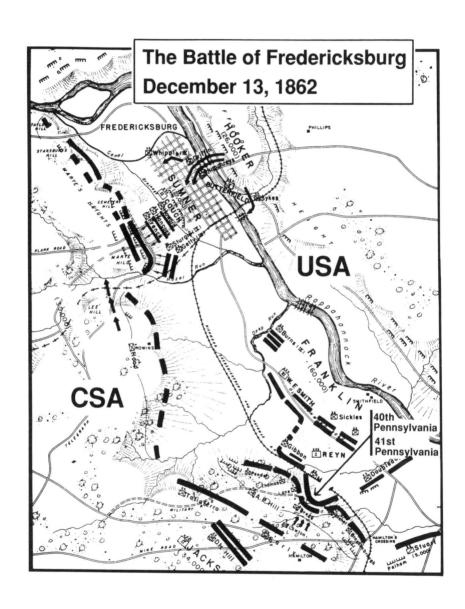

The Battle of Fredericksburg
December 13, 1862

against Lee, the first on the left of the Union army, southeast of Fredericksburg along the river. With the first assault, under the command of General William B. Franklin, Burnside hoped to roll up Lee's flank while the second assault through the town threatened Lee's entrenchments on Marye's Heights.[47]

Franklin's troops numbered 50,000 men, but it was the Pennsylvania Reserves, now only 4,500 strong, that was designated to lead the charge against the Confederate line. The Indiana County soldiers in the 40th and 41st Pennsylvania Regiments, once again, found themselves playing a major role in battle. Once across the Rappahannock River, the Pennsylvanians had to cross a railroad track and cultivated fields before they reached the sloping, forested heights where the rebels lay. The attackers were in full view of the defenders, and common sense would have dictated a different plan. But the Pennsylvanians launched a spirited attack at 2:00 p.m., drove through the rebel skirmishers at the railroad and in the fields. After two hours of hard fighting the Pennsylvanians gained the summit and pierced the Confederate line. They had accomplished exactly what Generals Burnside and Franklin had hoped. Unfortunately, other federal units did not advance as well and the Pennsylvanians found themselves covered on three sides beyond the Confederate line. Running low on ammunition and with heavy casualties, the Pennsylvanians came under heavy attack from Confederate reinforcements. They had to withdraw and surrender the coveted ground they had secured. As they retreated they had to abandon many wounded and isolated soldiers who became prisoners; among those left behind and subsequently captured was the "fighting parson," A. J. Bolar, who had been shot in both legs. Bolar was taken to Libby Prison outside Richmond where he lay for three months. He later reported that a Confederate surgeon thought both legs should be amputated "but they thought I would only live a short time and it was hardly worth while to amputate." The practice of both sides exchanging prisoners allowed Bolar to escape a long imprisonment. But his wounds were so debilitating that he was discharged from the army on January 30, 1864. Samuel Carbaugh, the young Brush Valley farm boy, also was severely wounded in the battle. Weakened by a bullet that pierced his right lung, he lamented to his parents that "You must not expect i can do much if i return home for i am very poorly. . . ." Carbaugh died at home on May 1, 1863.[48]

The failure of General Franklin to support the Pennsylvanians' breakthrough put an end to the battle on the eastern Confederate flank. The focus of the battle shifted to the assault against Marye's Heights where the Union army met entrenched Confederate artillery and riflemen. Fredericksburg, like so many previous battles, ended in stalemate and failure for the Union army.

The battle of Fredericksburg ended the first year of fighting for the Army of the Potomac. The campaigns which began with a massive movement against Richmond had seesawed back and forth across the Virginia and Maryland countryside. Yet, the shocking result was the severe casualties suffered by both sides. The battles had decimated the ranks of entire units. The Pennsylvania Reserve division which had played an instrumental role in the eastern campaigns was down to one-third of its original complement from 1861, and had to be retired to guard duty outside Washington.[49]

Throughout 1862 the horror of war reached back to Indiana County after each battle. The *Register* lamented after the Peninsula Campaigns: "It makes the heart sick to think of the terrible slaughter and sufferings of our brave soldiers. . . ."[50] After the battle of Second Bull Run, the editor bemoaned: "This county has again suffered severely."[51] Shocking to the citizens back in Indiana County were the lists after lists of relatives and friends who were now among the killed, wounded or missing. By the end of 1862, 143 of the nearly 2,000 Indiana County volunteers and draftees had died from disease, wounds, or battle fire. This represented an attrition rate of 7.1 percent.[52] In comparison to the deaths in particular battles, this attrition rate seems small, but one must consider that in 1861–1862, as the boys went off to war, few people thought in terms of losing seven percent of the county's soldiers.

Equally shocking was the evidence of demoralization among the Indiana County soldiers. Jack McClain, the twelve-year-old drummer boy of the 105th, quickly found the war more horrifying than he had earlier romanticized it to be. After the Peninsula Campaign, he appealed to Secretary of War Edwin Stanton for a special discharge. Stanton, knowing quite well that the battlefield was no place for a boy, granted the discharge and awarded young Jack a new brass drum.[53] Other volunteers had become disenchanted with the war. E. R. Brady in the Pennsylvania Reserves wrote home that soldiers were asking why they were fighting. They regarded the Confederate army as better organized and motivated while the Union army was demoralized, lacking in discipline, and beset with jealous generals. Brady had been in the army for sixteen months and had gone through four battles "and still I am unable to say what it all has been for." He wrote that he was contemplating resigning from the army. Shortly after he wrote this letter home to his parents, Brady was killed in the battle of South Mountain.[54] The demoralization and despair were evident in other reports from the field. E. E. Lewis, in the 78th Pennsylvania, wrote his cousin: "I tell you have no idy the hard stepts the soldiers has till you would try it and if you are sharp you will stay at home you have a good home and for god's sake stay there"[55] John C. Rugh, in the Blairsville contingent of Company E, 40th Pennsylvania, counselled a friend at home: "Mart, take a fools advice and never cum out in the army unless you hafte cum this war is a dambd humbug."[56]

Daniel S. Porter, commander of Company B, and one of the original enthusiastic recruits from Indiana County by late 1862, comprehended more correctly the meaning of battle. Reporting to Tom Moore's father of the death of his son at Antietam, Porter cried, "I feel lost. My brave comrades are falling around me . . . Loughry and Shambaugh fell at Bull Run. Stuchel, Wm. Loughry and Kimberlin at South Mountain. Your son and four wounded men in the last."[57] Certainly Porter would agree with the veteran, who many years later said of his enlistment day that it "was the morning of our lives, only we were solemn, all ignorant of coming events."[58] The campaigns of 1862 had introduced the reality of war to the enthusiastic volunteers and the countians back home. The subsequent trials of the Union called upon their resilient faith in the nation and their community to further sustain the effort.

☆ CHAPTER 3 ☆

THE COMMUNITY FINDS MORE SOLDIERS

"Is Indiana county less patriotic than her sister counties?" asked August Row, editor of Indiana County's Republican newspaper, the *Indiana Weekly Register*, in July 1862. "The crisis is upon us," he pleadingly continued. "The soldiers already in the field send their appeals and requests that they be reinforced speedily."[1] A week later "A WORKING MAN" answered Row's plea. Complaining that lawyers and propertied members of the community made fine recruiting speeches, but failed to enlist he asked "whether the *big bugs and rich men* haven't as much interest in the struggle as we have? It seems to me that the more property a man has, the more interest he has in putting down the rebellion . . . I prefer to wait for the draft, and take my chance with the rest."[2] As Row urged recruits to enroll in the army, contrary opinions demonstrated that patriotism in Indiana County, as well as throughout the nation, was waning in 1862. The terrible bloodletting of 1862 battles on the Peninsula, at Bull Run, and Antietam purged soldiers and citizens alike of their romantic visions of war and distilled their intense patriotism.

Yet President Lincoln and the War Department in the midst of the defeats of 1862 realized that the army needed a continual infusion of new men. The enthusiastic response of 1861 proved to be inadequate to meet the challenges of the rebellion. If the Union was to be maintained, Northern society had to achieve a state of full mobilization. More men needed to come forth, and communities throughout the North had to sacrifice their resources for the Union. In the spring and early summer of 1862, governors wary of dismal battlefield news urged communities to continue with recruitment. War meetings were held, communities offered financial inducements for new recruits, and newspaper editors called for a renewed vigor in recruiting. John S. Gibbons wrote his optimistic verses "We are

34

coming, Father Abraham, three hundred thousand more," but the response in 1862 failed to match the enlistments of the previous year.[3]

By the summer of 1862, with the Union army defeated outside of Richmond and recruitment slackening, President Lincoln resorted to desperate measures to find more manpower for the armies. The president called upon the governors to furnish him 300,000 additional recruits, the War Department authorized the payment of a $25 bounty to volunteers, and, finally, Congress on July 17, 1862, enacted the Militia Act. This legislation defined the militia as comprising all men between the ages of eighteen and forty-five, and authorized the president to call state militia into federal service for nine months. The War Department followed this act on August 4 with a call for 300,000 nine-month militia. With this action, the Lincoln administration had introduced a preliminary draft.[4]

Four days after Congress passed the Militia Act, Governor Andrew Curtin of Pennsylvania responded with a proclamation. "Everything that is dear to us is at stake," he said. "You have to save your homes and your firesides, your own liberties and those of the whole country." He called upon the counties to provide men for twenty-one new regiments and assigned each county a specified number of men to provide. He required Indiana County to provide two new companies, approximately two hundred men.[5]

In order to avoid the institution of a draft system in Indiana County, recruiting activities increased in the ensuing weeks. But the recruiting meetings met a lagging response. The very popular, young Republican Harry White, a major in the 67th Pennsylvania, came home to recruit and found only twenty-eight enlistees. Lieutenant Hannibal Sloan, still suffering from typhoid fever that he had contracted in the previous November, returned to Indiana County on a medical leave to find reinforcements for the battered Company B of the 40th Regiment. He, like Harry White, met apathetic responses.[6] The enlistees were so scarce that Republicans in the county feared that the community would not meet Governor Curtin's call. With the news of defeats and deaths coming in from the battlefield and the failure of the community to respond to the new calls, demoralization set in among the county's Republicans. "There is no use in concealing the fact that this is the darkest day the country has experienced since the commencement of the war," lamented Row of the *Register*.[7]

Seeing that patriotic appeals had failed to stimulate volunteering, the county turned to financial inducements to attract new recruits. The county commissioners offered a bounty of $30 to every volunteer who signed up to meet the county's requisition. With the county's $30, a federal bounty of $25, a mustering fee of $22, and one month's advanced pay equalling $13, a recruit could immediately pocket $90. That amount equalled about three months' pay for the ordinary laborer in the 1860s. Urging recruits to come forth before the August 10 draft deadline, Row at the *Register* appealed to their sense of patriotism, democracy, and self-interest: "Come on, all ye brave soldiers. The country needs your services. You will receive more pay than any soldiers ever received. Don't wait to be drafted. Volunteer and have a part in choosing your officers."[8]

It was not entirely the lack of patriotism or a sense of demoralization that deterred volunteers. To some degree, the men saw the need to attend to the cycles of agrarian life; they had to harvest their crops before they could leave home. Many were able to complete the harvesting early, and between August 6 and 8 they began to pour into Indiana to enlist. By Friday, August 8, sufficient volunteers enrolled to form three companies of nine-month recruits, and with approximately one thousand citizens bidding them goodbye at the railroad station, they left for military duty. These soldiers joined two nine-month regiments, the 177th Pennsylvania and the 135th Pennsylvania. The 177th, with Hugh Brady of Indiana County as a lieutenant colonel, guarded naval facilities near Norfolk, Virginia. The 135th included James R. Porter, formerly of the Indiana Guards, as colonel of the regiment, and Sam Nicholson, John G. Wilson, and John Kinter as captains of companies. This regiment served on guard duty outside of Washington, but Porter repeatedly requested combat duty. Consequently the 135th joined the Army of the Potomac at Fredericksburg and served as sharpshooters defending Union batteries during the battle.[9]

Despite the outpouring of volunteers in mid-August Indiana County had not fully met its obligations. The county's quota was 1,992 men and though 1,690 Indiana Countians were serving in the army, the county needed to find 302 additional men from a draft. Consequently, a new military system appeared in Indiana County for the first time. The 1862 Militia Act required that all able-bodied men between the ages of 20–45 be enrolled in the militia. That pool of men would then serve as the basis for drafting additional people to meet the county's quota. Unlike later "draft" laws, this militia draft was locally controlled and operated. August Row, editor of the *Register*, was appointed the enrolling officer and I. W. Watt served as the commissioner of the draft.[10] Rather than depending upon the "citizen volunteer," so characteristic of the American past, an imposed corporate system would determine now who would enter the military and who could remain at home.

The draft procedure, which began on September 4, stirred up heated controversy in Indiana County. "The great topic of discussion on all the streets and in the businesses is the draft," reported August Row, and he, with expected biases, said, "Everyone gives their approval."[11] For supporters of the war effort the draft could not have come at a more inopportune time. The 1862 draft procedure began as the bad news of Second Bull Run and Antietam, with the grisly lists of dead and wounded, was trickling home. At the same time President Lincoln boldly asserted emancipation as a war aim. Additionally, the congressional elections were taking place throughout the nation. Governor Curtin obviously was worried that the draft and other events might adversely affect the Republican candidates' chances in the autumn election. Correspondents around the state were warning the governor of the dire impact that the draft would have on the elections. "The postponement of the Draft will add five hundred majority in Montgomery County" to the Republican ticket, advised one writer. Curtin, therefore, postponed the draft until October 16, a week after the state elections. He explained somewhat lamely that he wanted to give everyone a chance to vote in the election.[12]

The 1862 congressional elections tested the will of Republicans nationally, in Pennsylvania, and in Indiana County. The elections revealed the skepticism about the war that was emerging throughout the nation. Exploiting the doubts about the war, the Democratic Party won important victories in New York, New Jersey, Illinois, and in Indiana. In Pennsylvania, the Democrats gained seats in the General Assembly, and won four additional congressional seats. The Democrats scored a victory in the 21st Congressional District, which included Indiana, Westmoreland, and Fayette Counties. John L. Dawson became the new congressman from this district. In Indiana County, the Democratic strength increased totally by only five percent, but the party showed a new vitality in some areas.[13]

The draft results, as well as the election tallies, reflected the waning support for the war. Row and Watt found only 177 soldiers with volunteers, draftees, and substitutes, giving the county a deficiency of 125 men. Additionally, the newspaper columns listed scores of citizens who were exempt from the draft. Enrolled citizens had claimed exemption on the basis of disability, age, or that they had vital positions such as postmaster and school director. Another feature of the system which spoke of the ebbing enthusiasm for military service was the appearance of drafted men with their substitutes, and a "want ad" in the *Register* for substitutes at $150. Additionally, the issue of religion was raised as ten men claimed exemption as conscientious objectors to the war.[14]

Just as the campaigns and the bloodletting continued so did the need to find soldiers. By 1863 volunteering throughout the Union and Pennsylvania as well as in Indiana County nearly disappeared, but the ongoing problem of finding military manpower had to be resolved. Congress had no recourse but to enact on March 3, 1863, the first federal conscription, or draft, in American history. This act shifted the authority for finding soldiers from local and state hands to the national government. It created draft boards to oversee congressional districts and to enroll every male between the ages of 20 and 45. From that list, the drafting officials would select by secret ballot enough men to meet the district's quota. Certain causes for exemption, such as failing to pass a physical examination, allowed drafted men to escape military service. But the most provocative aspects of the law allowing exemption from military service were "commutation" and "substitution." Commutation allowed a drafted person to avoid military duty if he paid a fee of $300. Or, one could escape the draft if he could find a substitute to go for him.[15]

The draft became the Civil War's most controversial piece of legislation. Opponents claimed the draft was unconstitutional, that commutation and substitution principles favored the rich over the poor, and that the system was replete with fraud. Resistance to the draft was also grounded in the American tradition of localism. By supplanting local and state procedures with a federal system the draft represented a step towards a modern nation which many people in the nineteenth century—and still in the late twentieth century—could not accept.[16] American citizens, then as now, disliked the encroachments of federal authority on their local interests and daily habits. Opposition to the draft was widespread and took many forms. Throughout the North, antiwar Democrats counseled resistance and stymied the drafting process. In New York City and in the Irish districts in Schuylkill and Lebanon Counties of Pennsylvania drafting officers met violent resistance.[17]

Indiana, Westmoreland and Fayette Counties comprised the 21st Draft District with its headquarters in Greensburg. Captain William B. Coulter was the provost marshal in charge of administering the draft system for the district. Coulter, a physician from Latrobe, had recruited and captained Company K of the 53rd Pennsylvania Regiment. Wounded at the battle of Fredericksburg, and having had his right arm amputated three inches from the shoulder, Coulter resigned his command to become the provost marshal.[18] August Row of the *Indiana Weekly Register*, formerly the enrolling officer for the 1862 Militia Draft, assumed a comparable role as the commissioner of the federal draft. Coulter and Row began the work of the draft board on May 1, 1863. They created a staff to assist them which included Dr. Fred G. Robinson, as the examining surgeon, William Coleman of Indiana and D. M. Springer of Uniontown as clerks, and Samuel H. Johnston of Indiana County and George I. Kellam as deputies. They divided the district into subdistricts (Indiana County had 31 subdistricts), appointed enrolling officers, and began the work of meeting the draft stipulations.[19] They designated the quotas for each county and its subdistricts based on the number of men enrolled in those areas. One of Row's constant tasks was to refine the enrollment lists as more men became twenty years old and thereby eligible. Additionally, he and his staff had to deal with erroneous information. Not atypical was the case of a young man from Cherry Tree who claimed ineligibility for the draft because he was not yet twenty years old. His mother and father testified "under oath" that their son had given his correct age, and the board removed the young man's name from the list of eligible draftees. Citizens in the family's neighborhood, however, contested the exemption and presented evidence that the young man and his parents had lied about his age. The board subsequently arrested him and held him for military duty.[20]

By July 1, 1863, Row completed the first enrollment for the district. His list totaled 3,879 eligible men for Indiana County, and the county's quota was 675 men. One would have anticipated that finding enough qualified men to meet the quota would have been easy. On July 13 Coulter, Row, and their staff met in the Indiana Court House to inaugurate the district's draft. A large crowd, males and females, attended the first drawing to see how this new procedure would work. Curiosity compelled some to attend, but others showed up because they believed "that a partiality would be manifested, and that political friends would be favored." Procuring the wheel that was used to draw jurors for trials, Coulter and Row dumped in the forms with the enrolled men's names, and turned the wheel several times. A blindfolded veteran reached into the chamber and pulled out the names one by one. As the veteran drew each name, he gave it to Coulter who announced the draftee's name, and Row recorded the drawing in the enrollment books. Altogether the veteran drew out 767 names from a barrel, nearly 100 more names than appeared necessary.[21] Coulter and Row apparently anticipated problems.

If so, their assumptions were quickly justified. Inklings of opposition to the draft appeared immediately. Two days after the draft five Indiana County draftees presented substitutes. Four of the substitutes, John Harvey, James Clark, John Jackson, and Robert Clark, were blacks or mulatto laborers in Indiana Borough. Obviously the original Indiana draftees had planned well in advance of avoiding military service and had hired the blacks. A War Department circular prohibiting the acceptance of blacks as substitutes foiled their plans, but the draftees quickly found other substitutes.[22] Yet, the acceptance of blacks was only a small problem compared to the further difficulties the draft officials encountered.

For the next two months Coulter and Row were consumed with claims that individuals were improperly enrolled, that parents were dependent for their livelihood on the young draftees, or that physical disabilities prevented one from entering the service. Dr. Robinson examined the men and disqualified 185 as physically unable to serve. The most frequent medical problems included hernias, lack of teeth, "piles," "under size," and consumption. One hundred and seventy-eight men paid the $300 commutation fee, thus contributing $53,400 to the nation's coffers. Coulter said that "almost every drafted man who could raise the money did so rather than enter the army." Sixty-eight men hired substitutes to go to war for them. The board granted others an exemption because they were thirty-five years old and married; and, forty-six men failed to report. When all the exemptions had been granted, protests heard, and commutation money accepted, the board had sworn into the service only 201 men.[23]

That this Republican stronghold, which heretofore had supported the war effort so vigorously, could barely provide only 32 percent of its quota was evidence of problems within the county. In Indiana County and the nation at large the draft system clearly lacked popular support. "The men now some of them are looking down in fact about it," observed one person.[24]

Yet, finding soldiers remained a national need and a local obligation. Worried about the problem, Indiana County leaders, including the Republicans, A. W. Taylor, William M. Stewart, Thomas St. Clair, and Democrat chieftain Silas Clark, met in the county courthouse on December 8, 1863, to consider ways to encourage enlistments. They realized that some financial inducement was necessary to encourage volunteers to step forward. Consequently, they adopted resolutions asking the citizens in a special poll to authorize the county commissioners to appropriate $150,000 for new recruits and $200,000 for veterans to re-enlist.[25] This meeting represented a major change in Indiana County's position on recruitment. Heretofore, the county had relied on "individualism" in the form of volunteering to answer the nation's need; but, in 1863, it was evident that "corporate" tools such as community appropriations were necessary to enlist soldiers. Subtly, the character of the Civil War was changing and affecting communities like Indiana County. Corporate power in the form of the draft and bounties was replacing the values of individualism and volunteerism.

Indiana Countians voted in the special poll on Saturday, December 19, and revealed that they were not ready to accept corporate authority over individual prerogative. Only 511 people voted whereas a month earlier in the gubernatorial race 5,916 people had voted. Yet the voters clearly sent a message to the county leaders. The vote was 161 to 350, a resounding defeat for county appropriations.[26]

With the county government denied the authority to offer bounties for volunteers, various townships decided to collect money from private donations and offer rewards to recruits. Cherry Tree, which needed only to find two men to meet its quota, quickly paid a bounty to two men to volunteer. Saltsburg collected $900 for volunteers and five men enlisted. Indiana Borough, which had to meet a quota of 13 men, quickly raised $1300 through private donations. As one might suppose, the various townships found themselves competing with one another for recruits. Young men volunteered to serve the township which offered them the best bounty. White Township paid for recruits from Washington and Center Townships; East Mahoning "bought" recruits from Montgomery township; and Indiana Borough took men from Blairsville and Burrell Townships.[27]

While some subdistricts earnestly sought recruits, Coulter reported that "others are doing little or nothing in that respect, seemingly, content that a Draft should take place."[28] The district received some assistance in meeting quotas as veterans returned home to bolster their depleted units. Daniel Porter and Archibald Stewart returned to Indiana County to find reinforcements for the 40th Pennsylvania. Veterans in Jacob Creps's Company A, 61st Pennsylvania re-enlisted in the field and when they came home on furlough they received local bonuses. The re-enlistment of veterans allowed the various subdistricts to receive credit and meet their quotas.[29]

The difficulty of raising troops and money for bounties was a statewide problem. To assist the local districts, the General Assembly enacted a Bounty Bill in March 1864, authorizing county commissioners or school directors to borrow money and levy taxes for bounties not exceeding $300.[30]

Indiana Borough quickly utilized the new state law to find soldiers. Indiana's town council authorized a loan of $1800 for bounties. It promised that each volunteer would receive a minimum bounty of $200. The response to Indiana Borough's offer was quick. Within a week the borough had enough recruits to meet its quota and avoid a draft.

Among those who took advantage of the bounty system were the Bronson brothers, members of an African-American family living in Burrell Township, the southernmost area of Indiana County. James Bronson, a twenty-five-year-old black, had enlisted a year earlier in the 5th Regiment, United States Colored Troops, on July 4, 1863 in Trumbull County, Ohio. Now, in 1864, his brothers,

George (age 23), John (age 18), and Noah (age 17) Bronson enlisted as recruits for Indiana Borough on April 13 and April 15, and were assigned to black regiments. Later, on August 25, John Patterson, a black from Greensburg, took advantage of the $100 bounty offered by Burrell Township and enlisted. Four days later, Thomas Bronson, a thirty-three-year-old laborer, followed his family members as an enlistee for Burrell Township.[31] An interesting and telling aspect of their story is that the Indiana County press gave them no attention. August Row, a staunch Republican whose party was supporting emancipation and the enrollment of blacks, made no mention of the Indiana County blacks who now joined the army. His comment in late April in the *Register* simply was that Indiana Borough had met its quota.[32] The African-American community in Indiana County, as in much of America, remained hidden and ignored beneath the surface of life.

As Indiana Borough and other subdistricts were attracting recruits with the bounties, Blairsville encountered a tide of anti-war sentiment. When Blairsville's town council authorized the school directors to borrow $5,000 in order to fund the bounties, they were halted temporarily by a group of thirty-eight citizens led by Dr. William R. Speer. Opposed to the draft and the bounty system, Speer and his associates did not want to pay any taxes to finance the system. They filed for an injunction in the county's Court of Common Pleas to prohibit Blairsville's officials from negotiating and issuing bonds for the bounty money. Speer, represented by the Democratic lawyers, Silas Clark and Hugh Weir, argued that Blairsville's action violated the 1857 Pennsylvania Constitution and thereby was unconstitutional. The issue, on which the suit was based, was a constitutional prohibition against municipal and county governments from incurring debts for corporations, institutions, or parties. This constitutional limitation clearly was intended to prevent a recurrence of local funding in road, canal, and railroad companies that had resulted in bankruptcy in the 1830s and 1840s. Now, the Speer suit argued, local indebtness for individual war bonuses violated the 1857 constitutional limitation. At the court hearing in late August, however, Judge Joseph Buffington argued that no relationship existed between the bounties and the constitutional prohibition, and dismissed the injunction. Speer appealed the local decision and carried the suit all the way to the Pennsylvania Supreme Court.[33]

The Civil War raised fundamental constitutional issues and *Speer et al. vs. Blairsville School Directors* (1865) placed Blairsville and Indiana County in the midst of the constitutional debate. During the Civil War conservatives, usually Democrats, objected to President Lincoln's extension of federal power. In a variety of federal cases and in political elections, they tried to counter the trend toward expansive federal authority. In Pennsylvania the conservatives controlled the state supreme court until 1864 and used their power to oppose the war and the Lincoln administration. For example, the state supreme court ruled that the 1863 draft was unconstitutional and it appeared that a contretemps between Pennsylvania and the federal draft officials might occur. The election of a Republican, Daniel Agnew, to the court allowed the new court to overturn the decision in 1864.[34] The Speer case was another example of the political and constitutional divisions of the Civil War era in Pennsylvania and the nation.

The Speer case clearly delineated the unfolding liberal and conservative constitutional thought of the day. Its focus very clearly was on the issue of limitation of power. The conservative argument given by Speer's lawyers and Justice James Thompson was sprinkled with the term "limitations." "The chief, if not the only object of written constitutions," Thompson argued, "is to limit the powers of government. . . ."[35] From that premise, then, the conservatives could attack Blairsville's action and the 1864 Bounty Bill. The 1857 state constitution limited local municipalities, like Blairsville, from contracting debts for persons or corporations. "Bounties and gratuities to soldiers are patriotic and commendable," said Thompson, "but it is not a legitimate purpose of a township, ward, or borough to create debts for any such object."[36]

This line of thought allowed the conservatives to maintain that state authority was limited from encroaching upon the responsibilities of the national government to raise armies and fight wars. "The harmony of our complex . . . government is only to be preserved by a strict regard to the operation of its parts, within their assigned limits."[37] Yet, the state bounties created a separate system of raising armies.

The conservatives also argued that military service of the citizen was his duty "pay or no pay." The bounty system, however, enabled the citizen to evade his duty and resulted in a tax on the community. It was a "startling assumption to claim that the community," Justice Thompson announced, "are bound to contribute money . . . to enable him to escape the service altogether!"[38] The bounty relieved the ordinary citizen from a "*debt he owes* the country, and the community pays for it."[39] The bounty was obviously a tax for private not public purposes.

The defense of Blairsville's school directors illustrated the liberal thought of the Civil War with its emphasis on community responsibility. Justice Daniel Agnew, the newest addition to the Pennsylvania Supreme Court, defended Blairsville's right to negotiate loans for the bounties. He began his argument by saying that "this is be-yond comparison the most important cause that has ever been in this court since the formation of the government."[40] The bounty is not a private transaction but a means to relieve the community of a burden, "a contribution from the public treasury for a general good."[41] Similar bounties were given, he noted, by communities to those who scalp panthers and wolves, destroy crow and blackbirds, capture horse thieves, or to aid hospitals and agricultural societies. In all instances, individuals benefit, but the community's interests are served.

Yet, the question of whether the bounty violated the Constitu-tion of 1857 had to be answered. Justice Agnew said the bounties did not conflict with the state constitution because the object of the money is not "*for* the *volunteer*, but for the community, which is to be relieved *by* the volunteer."[42] The person who received the bounty was not even known until he chose to step forward and volunteer. The public welfare is served further by the bounty, for the draft may take "the most valuable, useful, and needed mem-bers of society, whose extradition may produce the greatest injury and the most distress" to the community.[43] Raising money for the bounty was not obtained for any party or individual, but for the welfare and happiness of the community.

Agnew felt compelled to answer the argument that the bounty law encroached upon federal responsibility. No clause exists in the Constitution, he staunchly argued, "by which the right of self-pro-tection is taken away from the states."[44] "Who has forgotten the mighty shock of arms at Gettysburg, when the whole power of the nation was held in doubtful conflict . . . and when, for three anx-ious days, prayers ascended to the God of battles, and loyal men held their breaths, uncertain upon which side the victory had settled?"[45] In light of that experience, he concluded by saying that Pennsylvanians should pause before they stood on too narrow con-stitutional grounds.

By the time the Pennsylvania Supreme Court heard the argu-ments and handed down a decision on June 19, 1865, the war was over. Still, if the court had ruled in Speer's favor, he, his associates, and any Blairsville citizen could have refused to pay the taxes for the bounties. But, the court voted against Speer in a 3 to 2 decision.

While citizens in Blairsville balked and lawyers made their ar-guments, the draft and bounty system continued to operate in Indi-ana County. But the bounties failed to stimulate sufficient enlist-ments to satisfy Indiana County's quota and a second draft in June 1864 was necessary. Opposition, however, still persisted. Forty-five people paid the $300 commutation fee, 28 claimed exemptions for age or physical disability, and 9 failed to report. Throughout the district, draftees claimed exemption on the basis of religion. Provost Marshal Coulter was encountering "persons of very loose morals suddenly became converts" to the Dunkard denomination and claiming exemption. Only 5 men, one of them being a substitute, actually was mustered into service. Ironically, among the substitutes was sixteen-year-old Albert Gordon who enlisted for the commissioner of the draft and inveterate Republican—August Row. The county had failed to meet its quota by 74 people and a supplemental draft was set for the entire 21st District on September 5.[46]

Pressured by the prospects of another draft the people of western Pennsylvania raised their own troops rather than having the federal machinery do it for them. Coulter reported in mid-August that "recruiting in this District is very brisk at present . . . ." and that as the September 5 deadline for a draft approached the more energetic the people became in finding soldiers. "Recruiting offices in different parts of the District," he reported, "have been well patronized by Township and Borough committees, accompanied by squads of Recruits." Coulter encouraged volunteering by giving the volunteers their choice to which regiment they wished to be assigned.[47]

Indiana County was especially successful as it recruited enough men to form three new companies. Captained by T. J. Moore and J. A. Kinter of Marion, and William Brown of Marchand, and comprising about 250 men principally from the northern regions of Indiana County, the companies took the train in late August from Indiana to Pittsburgh. There they joined Colonel Hugh Brady's new regiment, the 206th Pennsylvania.[48]

Much to the chagrin of local citizens the war machinery demanded more troops in 1865. Lincoln issued another call. By this time the weariness with the war and the frustration with the recruiting and drafting had taken its toll even among the most enthusiastic supporters of the war like August Row. In a February 8 comment in the *Register* he charged that the quota system was fraught with errors and lambasted the Provost Marshal General James B. Fry for "the bungling manner in which [he] has so long managed the affairs of his office."[49] Across town James Sansom at the *Democrat*'s office equally condemned the draft. Sansom prophesied that a further draft would "sweep away every young able, bodied man and . . . put an end to farming operations." So objectionable was the draft, Sansom reported that it had replaced oil mania in the county as the topic of discussion. "The Draft," he said, "is all that is talked about."[50]

By 1865 many subdistricts created regular committees or associations to solicit recruits, and Indiana Borough was among them. The *Register* in an advertisement headed "THE DRAFT AND HOW

TO AVOID IT" called attention to James Turner, a recruiting agent in Indiana. The advertisement boasted that Indiana Borough's bounty was as large as any offered in the state and urged volunteers to step forward.[51] To meet the final call of the war for soldiers, citizens in the 21st District labored diligently and paid dearly to avoid a draft. Commissioner Coulter reported that recruiting was so active in February that he expected no draft would be necessary. Districts had been quite successful in finding volunteers by offering bounties between $300 and $500. Indiana Borough was among those districts paying a liberal bounty. To enlist 21 men the borough paid $11,000. The cost of finding recruits had climbed from $150 to $525 in the 21st District.[52]

As the story suggests money had replaced patriotism as the compelling motive of Civil War recruits. Apparently in Indiana County, sufficient men were still around to meet the draft quotas. They would come forth, however, only if financial inducements existed. These finances of the draft represented a major transfer of wealth during the Civil War. Northern society paid more than one-half billion dollars in bounty money. Some recruits shrewdly combined local and federal bounties to collect as much as $1,100.[53] In the 21st District, Coulter reported that the 1864 bounties alone totalled $1,210,350.[54] How much of that money in 1864 went into Indiana County is difficult to say; it is only necessary to imagine the money for all the bounties coming to the county's economy. For what was it used? Undoubtedly, some of it was squandered; but, a comment from Coulter suggested many recruits used their money wisely. "In many cases," he reported, "the sons give the money to their fathers to pay for their farms or invest for their own use hereafter."[55]

The bounty system invited fraud in western Pennsylvania as well as throughout the nation. Some draftees deserted from their townships and counties to enlist for bounties in other areas. Late in the war, February and March 1865, Coulter and Indiana County officials received reports that deserters from the Cambria County draft were enlisting as substitutes in Indiana County.[56]

Finally, one truly can see that the draft was the war's most divisive piece of legislation. It ripped apart community solidarity and turned patriotism to cynicism. Most Americans resented the imposition of an outside authority in determining who would go to war and who would stay home. The losses of individualism and local prerogative were tolls that few Americans wished to endure. Yet, the draft was a success in providing the Lincoln administration with the manpower it needed to maintain the Union. Provost Marshal Coulter, in his final report, expressed best the purpose of the draft, "the country had to be educated and brought forward rapidly. . . ."[57] Few can gainsay otherwise.

DANIEL S. PORTER
40th Pennsylvania
Palm Collection, USAMI

HANNIBAL SLOAN
40th Pennsylvania
Palm Collection, USAMI

ARCHIBALD W. STEWART
40th Pennsylvania
Palm Collection, USAMI

HUGH TORRANCE
40th Pennsylvania
Palm Collection, USAMI

48

RICHARD WHITE
55th Pennsylvania
Jerome Hunt Collection,
USAMI

THOMAS D. CUNNINGHAM
56th Pennsylvania
Civil War Library and Museum,
MOLLUS

JACOB CREPS
61st Pennsylvania
Palm Collection, USAMI

JOHN POLLACK
61st Pennsylvania
Palm Collection, USAMI

HARRY WHITE
67th Pennsylvania
Ronn Palm Collection, USAMI

WILLIAM CUMMINS
78th Pennsylvania
Palm Collection, USAMI

JOHN PARK BARBOR
135th Pennsylvania
Robert Barbor Collection, USAMI

JAMES MORROW
103rd Pennsylvania
Palm Collection, USAMI

50

MATTHIAS MANNER
105th Pennsylvania
Clarence Stephenson

JAMES BRONSON GRAVESITE
Photograph by Chuck Le Claize,
Courtesy of Allegheny County

ALEXANDER KELLY GRAVESITE

COMPANY B, 11TH REGIMENT P.R.V.C. REUNION AT BROOKVILLE, PENNSYLVANIA, SEPTEMBER 22, 1885

E. E. Allen   T. M. Coleman   H. C. Howard   W. N. Prothow

G. A. McLain   J. B. Hood   Samuel Shick   B. F. Laughlin   Capt. H. K. Sloan   H. Prothow   James Devlin

Harry Coleman   C. Schambaugh   Rev. T. Henderson   (Chill Laughlin)   John McCurdy   John Devlin

☆ CHAPTER 4 ☆

MEETING THE CRISIS OF THE UNION

By mid-winter 1863 August Row, editor of the *Weekly Regis-ter*, certainly sensed the rising disenchantment with the war. Ca-sualty lists were growing longer (Captain Creps reported 16 more dead in Company A, 61st Pennsylvania), petitions were circulating throughout Indiana County calling for a national convention to arbitrate the sectional differences, and criticisms of the Emancipa-tion Proclamation became more strident. Row's editorial on Febru-ary 24 called on Indiana Countians not to despair. "Many persons seem to think that the efforts of the Government to crush the re-bellion are on the wane, or rather that the rebellion is getting more powerful. We scarcely say that this notion is fallacious." The war was being won, it argued, the Union was being saved, and union-ists "are only more confirmed in their ideas and sympathies, and therefore emboldened."[1]

The mood in Indiana County at the outset of 1863 mirrored the mood throughout the nation. Defeat in the field, the injection of emancipation as a war objective, and the controversy over the draft deprived President Lincoln of the consensus he enjoyed in 1861 and early 1862. War weariness and desires for peace were dividing the country. For the Lincoln administration, the generals and the soldiers in the field, 1863 became the "crisis year." Victory or defeat on the battlefield this year would determine ultimately the direction of the war, and the strength of support for the war in communities like Indiana County. Perhaps Lincoln, like Row in Indiana County, realized that the Union was entering a pivotal year in the war against rebellion.

Throughout the year recruits, substitutes, and draftees from Indiana County continued to join the Union armies. By 1863 the local identification with companies waned as soldiers entered units recruited or organized throughout Pennsylvania or even other states.

Among the volunteers who enlisted in a non-Pennsylvania unit was James H. Bronson, the county's first African-American Civil War soldier. Bronson was born in Burrell Township in 1838, on the southern extremity of the county, where most of the African-Americans resided. He was not listed in the 1860 census for Indiana County and probably had moved to Pittsburgh. He enlisted on July 4, 1863, in the 5th Ohio Colored Troops, which was then being organized. How he became aware of that unit remains a mystery. Neither the Pittsburgh nor Indiana newspapers advertised for that unit. His service records reveal that he was a mulatto, 5' 9" tall, and a barber by occupation. He must have demonstrated strong leadership capabilities because he was immediately made first sergeant of his company. A few weeks later, on August 19, a second African-American who was born in Indiana County enlisted in the 6th Ohio Colored Troops. This was Alexander Kelly, who was born in 1840 in Conemaugh Township. By 1863 he had moved to Pittsburgh where he was employed as a coal miner. He, too, rose through the ranks to become the first sergeant of Company F.[2]

The special enrollment in 1862 of nine-month soldiers created two new regiments that included Indiana County volunteers. One regiment, the 177th Pennsylvania, with Hugh Brady of Indiana County as a lieutenant colonel, served on guard duty of naval facilities near Norfolk, Virginia and scoured nearby North Carolina marshlands and forests for guerrillas. Martin L. Bracken, a former school teacher and railroad clerk in Indiana County, served in Company K. Bracken's report after a scouting expedition in North Carolina revealed the lack of discipline in these specially raised regiments. Bracken wrote that his company "foraged on the citizens all along, destroyed a large store belonging to Mrs. Campbell. They just walked in and took all they wanted . . . I had no idea the 177th & especially Co K would pitch in so roughly . . . I must say some of our men could go up to a lady & take her Breast pin off her dress."[3] Also among the men in this regiment were recently drafted soldiers from Indiana County. One, John McNutt, a twenty-nine-year-old farmer from Brush Valley, had secured a position as an artilleryman at Fort Halleck near Suffolk, Virginia. He regarded this a better job because artillerymen only had to drill two hours a day. Infantrymen, on the other hand, drilled eight hours a day which "is enough to kill drafted men." The drafted men demonstrated stern recalcitrance to military duty. McNutt reported that in one Confederate attack on the fort a drafted regiment engaged in the fight only when "the cavalry chased them in." He and another Indiana Countian refused to take the oath when they were sworn into service. McNutt said he would never take oath and the army could send him home if it chose to do so.[4]

The second regiment, the 135th Pennsylvania, included James R. Porter, formerly of the Indiana Guards, as colonel of the regiment, and Sam Nicholson, John G. Wilson, and John Kinter as captains of companies. This regiment was assigned to guard duty in Washington, D.C. Here one of the young countians, Findley Carney, experienced one of his most memorable moments. He was guarding the White House one night in pouring rain. Suddenly he found himself facing the president. Mr. Lincoln ordered Carney: "Come in out of the rain." The young guard gratefully obeyed the commander in chief and years later claimed that Mr. Lincoln saved him from getting pneumonia.[5] Colonel Porter, however, wanted action, not tedious guard duty. He repeatedly requested that the 135th Pennsylvania be transferred to the Army of the Potomac. Needing troops the War Department transferred the 135th to the Army of the Potomac for the last battle of 1862, Fredericksburg, where they served as sharpshooters defending Union batteries.

While the year opened inauspiciously in the East, the Union army in the West engaged in a battle that began to change the course of the war. Indiana Countians in the 78th Pennsylvania played a bloody, but strategic, role in this western engagement, the battle of Stones River. Cummins' and Forbes' soldiers in the 78th Pennsylvania left their posts in Nashville on December 26, 1862, with General William S. Rosecrans to drive the Confederate army out of east Tennessee. The Confederates commanded a key railroad and turnpike location at Murfreesboro along Stones River. By December 30 the two armies faced each other astride the river just north of Murfreesboro awaiting orders to attack. Shortly after 6:00 a.m. on December 31 the Confederates attacked first. They launched an attack on the Union right but met a stubborn resistance. By noon, however, the Union right could no longer hold its position. The entire Union line collapsed back on the Union's other line, giving the army's position the configuration of a bent jackknife. In the center, or the hinge, and receiving attacks from three sides was the 78th Pennsylvania as part of Colonel John F. Miller's brigade. The Confederates believed this apex to be the weakest point in the Union line and attacked it fiercely. But the 78th Pennsylvania and its sister regiments held on until their ammunition was exhausted. Only then were they relieved and did retire to the rear. The Union line held the remainder of the day against repeated Confederate attacks that finally ended in late afternoon.

New Year's Day, 1863, broke cold and grim with both armies expecting a renewal of the fighting. But the day passed as soldiers cooked biscuits and rested, regiments gathered up the stragglers and lost, and medical personnel took care of the wounded and dead.

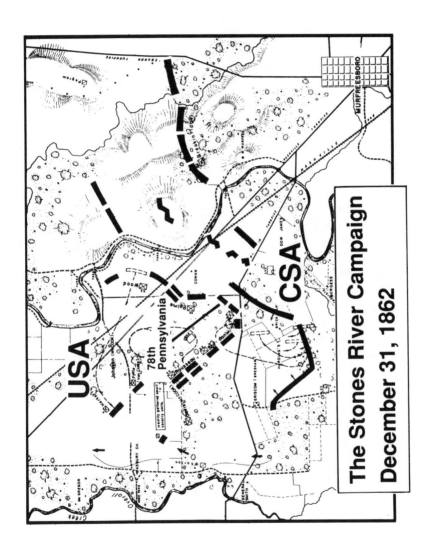

The Stones River Campaign
December 31, 1862

On January 2 fighting broke out anew as the Confederate army attacked the Union left. Miller's command with the 78th Pennsylvania had moved across the Stones River to support the Union left and found itself in the midst of the fighting again. Late in the day Miller's brigade was ordered to the front. With the 78th Pennsylvania, and Captain Cummins with the Chambersville volunteers, leading the way, Miller's brigade counterattacked a surging Confederate line. As the rebels halted and gave way, the 78th Pennsylvania, followed by Ohio, Indiana, Illinois, and Michigan regiments, pierced the Confederate lines and swooped down on the Confederate artillery. The 78th Pennsylvania captured a battery of cannons and the colors of the 26th Tennessee Regiment. The Confederates could no longer sustain themselves against the Union attacks and retreated. Rosecrans won his objective in capturing Murfreesboro. Indiana Countians shared in the laurels of the victory. Captains Cummins and Forbes, and Lieutenants William Maize and John Marlin received the commendations of their commanding officers.[6] Yet, the victory was a costly one. The Union army suffered 31 percent casualties (the Confederates lost 33 percent). Among the dead were 11 Indiana County soldiers.

While the western armies battled for strategic ground the eastern armies went into winter quarters. The Pennsylvania Reserves had suffered heavily in the 1862 campaigns and those regiments retired to guard duty outside Washington, D.C. With its ranks thinned the possibility for promotion opened for officers and enlisted men. Indiana County's Dan Porter and another captain, James Speer, competed for the open lieutenant colonelcy. Local politics played a role in the Civil War military, and both captains enlisted supporters to influence Governor Curtin in making the promotion. Harry White, still a state senator, personally solicited the governor on Porter's behalf explaining, "I am most interested in it as well my constituents." William M. Stewart, a Republican county commissioner for Indiana County, assured the governor that there was "no braver or more gallant man in the service than Capt Porter" and "he is a scholar and a gentleman perfectly correct in his habits a high credit to our county." Porter's case was no doubt enhanced by the political influence, but his service record was exemplary, too. When some units of the Pennsylvania Reserves had been captured in the Peninsula Campaign, Porter organized the remainder for regimental duty. Perhaps his competitor unwittingly strengthened Porter's claim by appealing to the governor's sympathy. Speer wrote that Porter "has never been wounded and never even been a prisoner while I have three times been wounded & a prisoner & must resign if I am not promoted as I am disabled by my wounds from performing the duties of a line officer." For whatever reason—politics, leadership, or health—the governor promoted Porter on May 14, 1863, as lieutenant colonel of the 40th Pennsylvania. Hannibal Sloan then became captain of Company B, 40th Pennsylvania, and Archibald Stewart was promoted to first lieutenant.[7]

With the spring of 1863 dawning, the Army of the Potomac emerged from its winter slumbers revitalized, with a new commander, "Fighting Joe" Hooker, and a new plan. Hooker determined that he would make a wide sweep to the west of Fredericksburg, cross various fords on the Rappahannock, outflank Lee's defenses, and rush towards Richmond. But Confederate scouts detected the movement of the Army of the Potomac and Lee moved his army to counter Hooker. The two armies collided once again just ten miles west of Fredericksburg at a little crossroads, Chancellorsville, deep in the Virginia forests.

The battle of Chancellorsville, May 1–3, 1863, warrants particular attention because it was Robert E. Lee's best battle. Working with Stonewall Jackson, Lee created a masterpiece of military strategy. On the second day of the battle, May 2, he allowed Hooker's forces to penetrate deep into the forests as Confederates withdrew. Lee then diverted 25,000 of his troops under Stonewall Jackson on a flanking movement against the left of Hooker's army. At 5:00 p.m. as the XI Corps of the Union army settled down to prepare their evening meal after what had been seen as a day of Union triumph, Jackson's men came crashing down on the Union troops. The men of the XI Corps fled and the left wing of the Union army collapsed. Only the onset of darkness and confusion in the overlapping lines prevented a true rout of the Union army.[8]

Indiana Countians, either as veterans, rookie volunteers, draftees, or nine-month soldiers, could be found in every area of this battle. Only those in the Pennsylvania Reserve were missing because that division was resting outside Washington.

Veterans from northern Indiana County in the 105th were positioned in the center of the Union line as part of the III Corps. On May 1 they formed a line near Chancellor House, receiving a heavy shelling from Confederate artillery. They were on the skirmish line the next day in the center of the Union line. That afternoon the 105th advanced to reconnoitre an enemy advance which was Stonewall's Jackson's force moving around the right of the Union army. The 105th encountered the rebel forces and then spent the night just south of Orange Plank Road. The next day, Sunday, May 3, the 105th engaged rebels on the left flank of the Union army around Hazel Grove. In this engagement Colonel McKnight, the regimental commander from Brookville, was shot through the head. The regiment retook the first line and held for two hours against rebel firing. Also among those killed was the thirty-three-year-old redhead Captain Robert Kirk, Company F, who had come with his folks from Ireland in 1843 to Canoe Township in Indiana County. Indiana Countians, James Silvis, Robert Doty, and George H. Reed, were among those who received a special citation, the Kearny Badge, for distinguishing themselves in this battle.[9]

The 56th Pennsylvania, which included McIntire's volunteers from Blairsville, served as a regiment in the 1st Corps guarding the U.S. Mine Ford on the Rappahannock.[10]

The 61st Pennsylvania, with Captain Jacob Creps and Company A from Indiana County, participated as part of the VI Corps. Its mission was to cross the Rappahannock, dislodge the rebels at Marye's Heights, and secure Fredericksburg. The 61st Pennsylvania was one of the units that led the assault. On May 3, a Sunday morning with no church bells pealing and no worshippers in evidence, the sun cleared off the fog. About noon the 61st Pennsylvania formed in column formation, with Company A in the lead, and advanced on enemy fortifications on the hills overlooking Fredericksburg. Private John A. Stewart, who had entered the 61st Pennsylvania in August, 1862, vividly remembered the charge as "something like a thunder storm, only many times greater; the roaring of cannon and the bursting of shells above our heads. . . ." The rush of the Union troops overcame Marye's Heights and by late afternoon the 61st Pennsylvania and other regiments in the VI Corps occupied the rebel ground. But while they had succeeded, Hooker at Chancellorsville had been outwitted by Lee and Jackson. The Union army was stalemated again and Hooker showed no resolve to renew the battle. Lee, learning that his position at Fredericksburg was lost, ordered reinforcements back to the town and, on May 4, they attacked the VI Corps. The Union troops could not hold the position and had to withdraw across the river. Captain Creps, of Company A, was wounded in the hand when a minie ball struck the handle of his revolver, and Private John A. Stewart was wounded in the left arm and taken prisoner. His brother, Henry, attempted to rescue him but he was also captured. Both were paroled in about eight days, and the Confederate surgeons used shingles to make a splint for Stewart's wounded arm. But when they released him they jokingly warned that "if I ever came back, they would take my arm off close up to the shoulder. . . ."[11]

A new three-year regiment, the 148th Pennsylvania, that had organized in late summer of 1862 and included forty-two Indiana Countians, experienced its baptism of fire in this battle. The Indiana County soldiers were from the Plumville area and included

Lieutenant John F. Sutton, who subsequently became captain of Company E. Serving in Hancock's II Corps, the 148th was at the Chancellorsville crossroads in the middle of the forests. The 148th was in the midst of the battle on May 2–3, and the regiment lost twenty-five men. None of the casualties included Indiana County soldiers.[12]

Another young regiment in this battle was the 135th Pennsylvania that included the nine-month volunteers who had left Indiana County the previous August. They were in Reynolds's I Corps on the extreme left of the Union line along the Rappahannock River. On May 2, Reynolds took his troops from its position east of Fredericksburg to the other extreme side of the Union army at Chancellorsville. Positioned there to reinforce the Union left, the 135th covered the front of the brigade. John Park Barbor, an Indiana County recruit in the 135th, worriedly wrote in his diary that his unit "occupy a position in rear of a Rifle pit said to be one of the most dangerous in an open field the rebs west of us in the woods." The inexperienced unit remained alert and cautious throughout the night, but no action occurred. The following morning, May 5, rebels charged from their wooded concealment, but the firepower of the 135th Pennsylvania and other units drove them back. Barbor noted that he had fired one shot of double grape and canister.[13]

Three weeks later, on May 24, 1863, the 135th's nine-month enlistment came to end. Barbor and the volunteers returned to Indiana aboard the midday train on May 27. They tried to return to the calm of civilian life, but their brief enlistment had introduced them to the realities of war and many felt an obligation to return to the field. Additionally they felt pressure from soldiers in the field and civilians at home who believed the nine-month enlistees had had it too easy. Barbor began a career as a science teacher in School No. 1 in Green Township. Throughout the winter, however, he mulled over his academic interests and his civic responsibilities. The latter prevailed and his diary entry for February 14, 1864 reads: "Enlisted yesterday at Indiana in the Signal Corps. Have to report on Tuesday the 23d."[14]

Finding more soldiers took on a sudden urgency in June 1863 as the Confederate army advanced northward into Pennsylvania. Governor Curtin issued a call for sixty thousand ninety-day soldiers to defend the Commonwealth against the menacing rebel invasion. No one knew Lee's destination and the fear of a rebel invasion gripped Philadelphia, Harrisburg, Altoona, and Pittsburgh. Fear of the invaders proved valid as the Confederate soldiers plundered the rich Pennsylvania countryside. The American people as well as the Constitution had become the target of the rebellion.[15]

Again Indiana County responded to the governor's call. Within a couple of weeks 1,100 men in sixteen companies from the county enlisted in the special militia. Row's *Weekly Register* especially called attention to First Lieutenant Robert Smith in Reverend Samuel Anderson's company from Young Township. Smith had already lost two sons in the war and two others were still in the army. Now Mr. Smith, like many other fathers, left his farm without male laborers to answer the nation's summons. The response was a bipartisan effort as noted by the Democratic leader Hugh Wier who led a company of sixty-nine volunteers.[16]

Samuel William Campbell and George W. Bolar, who had also served in the 135th Pennsylvania, were among those recruiting for militia in southern Indiana County. Campbell confided that he was not recruiting "so much as i thought for." Failing to find as many recruits as they hoped, they solicited volunteers at a schoolhouse near New Germany. "Great many of the boys would like to go along to the Army," Campbell observed, "if it were not for their parents." By Saturday, June 20, he and Bolar had found 43 recruits. They elected Dan Tinkcom, proprietor of the Union Hotel in Armagh, as captain, Campbell, first lieutenant, Bolar, second lieutenant. On the road to Camp Howe outside Pittsburgh, some recruits changed their mind and "played the slip on us along the way." Only 49 took the oath which allowed for only one commissioned officer which Campbell took. Tinkcom and Bolar returned to Indiana County to find more recruits. Tinkcom found enough men to advance the company to sixty men, and these recruits became six-month volunteers in Company F, 2nd Pennsylvania Battalion. They served as railroad guards along the B&O Railroad in western Maryland.[17]

In the path of Lee's northward march was Harry White's 67th Pennsylvania Regiment that he had recruited heavily from Brush Valley in early 1862. As chairman of the Republican Party in Indiana County he gained a political appointment from Governor Curtin as a major in the 67th Pennsylvania. Though he admitted that military service was his duty, political ambition was a controlling factor in his life. He obviously knew that he could not continue to be a leading Republican in Indiana County and avoid military duty. He wanted to command a regiment because "as good a position as possible is now to be desired." While the 67th was stationed in Annapolis guarding prisoners, White actively worked with Republicans back in Indiana County to get himself elected as a state senator representing Indiana and Armstrong Counties. His election caused some complications for he then had political and military duties to meet, but he chose not to resign from the army. "I do not see my way clear to go into civil life just now," he explained to his father, "& leave in the field so many men I have induced to go there with me."[18]

The 67th Pennsylvania transferred the following spring to reinforce Union defenses in the Shenandoah Valley. The regiment joined the VIII Corps under General Robert H. Milroy and was assigned to guard Berryville, a strategic point along the Shenandoah River just east of Winchester. "It is one of Jackson's haunts," wrote Harry White, "& my opinion is should a raid be made up this valley this point would be first attacked." His picket lines frequently clashed with rebel cavalry who obviously were testing the Union army's lines. Day by day the rebels grew bolder and began to raid supply wagons. One such clash resulted in the 67th Pennsylvania losing eleven men, including Robert Adams of Indiana who was captured. The anxiety level among the Union troops was building and White reported that his men "frequently sleep upon our arms."[19]

Had they known the Confederate plans and movements up the Shenandoah Valley in late May, White and his men would have been even more anxious. They and the rest of Milroy's command at Winchester were a principal target of Lee's II Corps. Formerly Stonewall Jackson's command, these tough veterans were now led by General Richard S. Ewell. His mission was to clear the Shenadoah Valley of Union troops. Lee then could march into Pennsylvania with no threat from a Union attack on his western flanks.

As the Confederate army reached the vicinity of Winchester around June 11 and 12, Milroy disbelieved reports that a major force threatened him. Nonetheless, he decided to consolidate his troops and called the brigade at Berryville into Winchester on Saturday morning, June 13. As the 67th Pennsylvania and the other troops hastily withdrew they left many tents, wagons, and foodstuffs which rebels quickly captured. White's troops joined the remainder of Milroy's command in the defense of Winchester where on June 14 they endured Confederate shelling and prepared for Confederate assaults on the town.[20]

The Confederates pounding on the town unnerved Milroy. Fearing that he would lose his entire force, Milroy ordered his troops to retreat to Harper's Ferry. In the morning darkness of June 15, the withdrawal began. The Confederates anticipated the retreat and sent infantry and artillery to Stephenson's Depot just north of Winchester to cut off Milroy's escape route. As Milroy's troops streamed up Martinsburg Pike they encountered the awaiting rebels. Repeated thrusts against the rebels failed and Milroy's army began to fall apart with individual units seeking a hasty exit from Winchester.[21]

The 67th Pennsylvania led their brigade's retreat up the Martinsburg Pike. About three miles north of Winchester they encountered rebel artillery on their front and shifted eastward for a possible flanking movement on the Confederate line. White's regiment moved onto a farm belonging to J. Easter and came upon the farmer's spring house. Suffering from thirst they stopped and the regiment lost its discipline. As one report noted they "ceased to be an organized regiment." Broken into small groups the 67th became easy prey for advancing Louisiana regiments. Frantically Harry White tried to warn the men: "Be ready boys, he may be here any moment." But White had lost control of the regiment and the Confederates quickly overwhelmed the disorganized 67th. All but 44 of its 700 men and officers were captured or killed. During the brief engagement White's horse stumbled into a ditch, fell, and threw White from the saddle. Crippled with an injured leg and shoulder, White was among those captured by the Louisiana Tigers Regiment. He and his men marched as prisoners down the valley to Staunton where they boarded railroad cars bound for Libby Prison in Richmond. Within a month the enlisted men were exchanged and paroled, but Harry White and the other officers remained behind as prisoners.[22]

While Harry White and the 67th Pennsylvania suffered the discomfort and indignity of Libby Prison, the Confederates advanced across the Mason-Dixon Line into the fertile farmland of Pennsylvania. The Union army, now under the command of General George Meade, gave chase to Lee's troops. Unexpectedly, both armies found each other at a sleepy hamlet, Gettysburg, on July 1, 1863.

As the two armies approached one another for that fateful battle, the 56th Pennsylvania, including the Blairsville Company, was in the I Corps, 1st Division, and Cutler's brigade that engaged the rebels northwest of the town. Immediately upon positioning themselves at a railroad cut to meet the rebels the 56th Pennsylvania and two other regiments came under fire. The 56th Pennsylvania returned the fire and became the first infantry unit in the Union army to fire a shot in the battle of Gettysburg. The Confederates gained higher ground and poured a heavy fire into the 56th Pennsylvania and its sister units. The Union troops had to withdraw to the woods on Seminary Ridge while the engagement shifted to other segments of the line. When the 56th Pennsylvania arrived at Gettysburg, they had 17 officers and 235 men in the regiment. In the first twenty minutes of the battle, they lost 70 killed and wounded. The following day, July 2, they engaged the enemy on the ridge in the rear of the town and lost 5 more men killed or wounded. Among those wounded at Gettysburg from the 56th Pennsylvania were Indiana Countians, Thomas D. Cunningham, Anthony Earheard, Henry Fox, and John Henderson. Indiana Countians killed in action or dying of wounds from Gettysburg included John W. Crusan, John D. Gordon, Robert Kelley, and Christian Ling.[23]

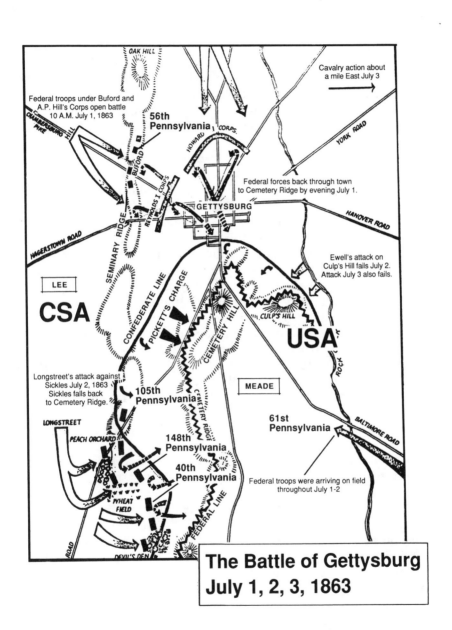

Cavalry action about a mile East July 3

Federal troops under Buford and A.P. Hill's Corps open battle 10 A.M. July 1, 1863

56th Pennsylvania

OAK HILL

CHAMBERSBURG PIKE

BUFORD'S

HOWARD CORPS.

YORK ROAD

REYNOLDS I CORPS.

GETTYSBURG

Federal forces back through town to Cemetery Ridge by evening July 1.

HANOVER ROAD

HAGERSTOWN ROAD

SEMINARY RIDGE

CONFEDERATE LINE

PICKETT'S CHARGE

CEMETERY HILL

CULP'S HILL

Ewell's attack on Culp's Hill fails July 2. Attack July 3 also fails.

LEE

CSA

USA

Longstreet's attack against Sickles July 2, 1863 Sickles falls back to Cemetery Ridge.

105th Pennsylvania

CEMETERY RIDGE

MEADE

61st Pennsylvania

ROCK

BALTIMORE ROAD

LONGSTREET

PEACH ORCHARD

148th Pennsylvania

40th Pennsylvania

Federal troops were arriving on field throughout July 1-2

WHEAT FIELD

FEDERAL LINE

ROAD

DEVIL'S DEN

The Battle of Gettysburg
July 1, 2, 3, 1863

As the two armies joined the initial units around Gettysburg, on the second day of the battle, July 2, Lee decided to attack the left of the Union line. On the extreme position of the Union army were two knolls, commonly known as the "roundtops." If the Confederates could occupy those hills, they could enfilade the Union line from high ground. Lee understood the strategic value of those heights and on July 2 initiated the contest for control of Little and Big Round Top. At 4:00 p.m. 15,000 screaming rebels under the command of General James Longstreet poured into the Devil's Den rocks and the Wheatfield.[24]

Daniel Sickles's III Corps, which extended in a salient from Devil's Den to the Emmitsburg Road, took the brunt of the attack. The 105th Pennsylvania, the Wild Cat Regiment, that included many Indianans, positioned itself at the junction of Emmitsburg Road and Trostle's Lane on the right side of the salient. To their left were other Pennsylvania units. As they awaited anxiously for an anticipated attack heavy artillery fire rained in on their position. Matthias Manner, a twenty-year-old farm boy from Deckers Point in Indiana County, in Company I, 105th, and a veteran since 1861, described the Confederate artillery barrage as "the hottest shelling I ever saw." Artillerists tended to agree; Edward P. Alexander, Longstreet's chief artillery officer, later said: "I don't think there was ever in our war a hotter, harder, sharper artillery afternoon than this." The rebel artillery fire took its toll among the Union line. The 105th suffered twelve casualties, including G. W. McHenry, of Indiana, who lost a leg. The federal troops bore this artillery fire for over an hour and then the rebels charged.[25]

The III Corps's salient proved to be undermanned for the Confederate assault. The left of the federal position gave in first and then the Confederates simply rolled up the remaining units along the Emmitsburg Road. The 105th was the last unit to hold the Union line; it met the charge of the rebels, joined with remnants of other units and counterattacked. The Pennsylvania "wildcats" drove the rebels back, and "fought like demons." But they could not hold the line against overwhelming odds and had to join their sister units of the III Corps in a general retreat. The 105th lost 132 men, killed, wounded or missing, nearly one-half of its men, in the fight, including the corps commander Daniel Sickles who was wounded and lost his right leg. From Indiana County among the soldiers killed was Sergeant Robert Doty, who had won the Kearny Badge at Chancellorsville.[26]

The II Corps under Hancock came forth to stem the rebel tide and its 1st Division, which included the 148th Pennsylvania and Company E from Indiana County, marched into the Wheatfield.

One of the 148th soldiers later remembered, "We were the first troops to cross the field, and the yellow grain was still standing. I noticed how the ears of wheat flew in the air all over the field as they were cut off by the enemy's bullets." The Union reinforcements clashed with the Confederates and for a brief time retook the Wheatfield. But, a new Confederate surge exhausted the Union soldiers and they began a scattered retreat towards the safety of Little Round Top and Cemetery Ridge.[27]

    Among the reinforcements on the Union Line was the Pennsylvania Reserve Division, now under the command of General Samuel W. Crawford. When the Pennsylvania Reserves learned that Lee had invaded Pennsylvania they petitioned to rejoin the army and defend their home state. General Meade also appealed to the War Department for the Pennsylvania Reserve and they were assigned to Sykes's V Corps. They left their Maryland site at 5:00 a.m. on July 1 and marched all day and night for Gettysburg. With only a two-hour break for sleep, the Pennsylvania Reserves reached the battleground in late afternoon and were brought into line to defend Little Round Top. The Reserves were divided with several regiments, including the 41st Pennsylvania, assigned to the higher ground on Little Round Top and other units stationed on the lower slope.[28]

    The 40th Pennsylvania was under the command of Colonel Samuel McCartney Jackson, a thirty-year-old merchant from Apollo, Pennsylvania. The regiment, including the Indiana County companies, positioned itself in the center of the defensive line at Little Round Top fronting on the Wheatfield and Peach Orchard with Devil's Den to the left. As Hannibal Sloan later remembered, they numbered only about 400 men. From that vantage point they saw the Confederate attack on the III Corps and became the target of artillery fire themselves. The Reserves hugged the ground and awaited the retreating Union soldiers of the III Corps to clear away. Then the Pennsylvanians raised up, fired two volleys, and with the 40th Pennsylvania in the lead, charged down the slopes of Little Round Top into what one famous painting called the "Valley of Death." They charged across the Plum Run at the bottom of the hill, drove back advancing rebels, and reached a stone wall at the edge of the Wheatfield. With bayonet and riflebutt they overcame Georgians and South Carolinians, and took the wall. Other Pennsylvanians soon joined them and by dusk the Federal left was secure. That night General Samuel Crawford, commander of the Pennsylvania Reserves, came down to the 40th Pennsylvania and told them they had saved the day. "Your regiment is worth its weight in gold; its weight in gold, sir!"[29]

The 41st Pennsylvania, which included Bolar's old company, was diverted to support the higher ridges of Little Round Top. That position came under ferocious attack from the Confederates, and the 83rd Pennsylvania and the 20th Maine held on to that strategic area. Nonetheless, the Pennsylvania Reserves reinforced the line late in the day and helped to stave off the remnants of the Confederate assault.[30]

Also rushing in to bolster the line around Little Round Top that evening was the VI Corps which included Creps's Company A, the 61st Pennsylvania. The 61st had been in Maryland, thirty-four miles away from Gettysburg, on July 1. Called upon by Meade to hurry to Gettysburg, the soldiers fell into line at dark and marched all night towards the battle site. Captain Creps was hobbled by an acute case of erysipelas in his leg. His leg was so inflamed that he could not wear his officer's boot and had to cover his foot with a cut-open shoe. A physician had advised amputation of the leg, but Creps refused to undergo the operation. Weary and hurting, he rode a horse and maintained the quick pace. Stopping only briefly for a short morning breakfast break, the 61st responded to Meade's repeated calls with hurried steps. Their march was so quick that many officers upon seeing the 61st arrive on the battlefield thought they were cavalry units. Panting and exhausted they reached slopes of Little Round Top after the charge of the Pennsylvania Reserve and served as a further evidence of the strengthened Union line. The next day they occupied four different places in the line and Captain Creps with four companies was on the extreme right of the Union line, continually engaged with Confederates all day.[31]

While Pennsylvania troops bore much of Pickett's famous charge on July 3, Indiana Countians, for the most part, were out of the area of intense fighting. Only Indiana's Company E, 148th Pennsylvania, participated in the defense of Cemetery Ridge. A Confederate brigade on Pickett's extreme right assaulted the position which the 148th defended. The withering fire from the Union lines broke the assault and many of the Confederates surrendered.[32] William Penn Oberlin, a Smicksburg enlistee, lay in the midst of the line and later described the battle to his wife:[33]

> about 2 o'clock fierce shelling began such a bursting of the shells as there was I cannot describe to you. I lay at the root of a small bushy tree, the shells bursted above and around me, killing men and horses. . . The shelling lasted about 2 hours, then ceased, and then came forward the lines of rebel infantry. I lay flat on the ground, until they came within range of my rifle, then I focused in shot after shot. . . I crawled forward some distance to a small pile of chopped wood. Here I had another

good chance of popping them. When they came pretty close to us picketts, our artillery pounded grape and canister into them, killing wounding and scattering them in all directions. . . Such that would run we would holler to come into our lines, if they refused we would shoot them if we could hit them. I dropped two of them at a distance of about two hundred and fifty yards. Another young fellow and I went out and brought in 7 prisoners.

The next day, July 4, as Indiana County's Matthias Manner noted in his diary, both armies gathered up the wounded and buried the dead. "Every thing has been quiet up to 9 o'clock," he wrote that night, "there hasnt been a shot fired on either side that I even herd."[34] Both armies knew they had fought a major battle in this agony of the American Republic.

Calm settled on the Eastern Theater after Gettysburg, but in the West the action intensified. Grant took Vicksburg on July 3, and Lincoln was hopeful of crushing the Confederacy with a third blow in Tennessee. General Burnside lived up to Lincoln's expectations by taking Knoxville on September 3, and General Rosecrans pushed towards the vital railroad center, Chattanooga.

Rosecrans took Chattanooga without a fight and pursued the Confederate army into northwest Georgia. There, along the Chickamauga Creek on September 20 his army barely escaped annihilation by a reinforced Confederate army. In this battle, General George H. Thomas plugged the Union line at a vital moment, winning for himself the nickname "Rock of Chickamauga." The Union army repulsed repeated Confederate attacks and retreated to the security of Chattanooga. Though the Confederates had won the battle, Rosecrans still held Chattanooga.

As Rosecrans's army moved south towards Chattanooga it was missing one of its popular officers. William Cummins of Chambersville, remembered by the regimental historian as "the very popular commander of Company A," 78th Pennsylvania, became too ill to command his company. With deep regret he had to resign his commission and left the army on August 5, 1863, to return home and recuperate. Other Indiana Countians remained as soldiers in the 78th Pennsylvania as part of General Negley's division. Fortunately for them, the 78th maneuvered considerably throughout the battle to reinforce various spots on the Union line. At various times they appeared to be in the heart of an upcoming engagement when they were ordered to move to another position on the Union line. At one point the 21st Ohio substituted for them and subsequently was cut to pieces. As a result the 78th missed the heat of most of the action and lost as few men as any regiment.[35]

Over the next several months the 78th and Rosecrans's army remained under siege in Chattanooga. The Confederates occupied the mountain heights and passes around the city and hoped to starve the Union army into submission. The Confederate stranglehold nearly succeeded. Soldiers robbed the corn designated for the horses and "the average soldier of the 78th Pennsylvania had a great deal of sympathy with the Children of Israel who, when in the Wilderness, remembered the flesh pots of Egypt."[36] By mid-October General Ulysses S. Grant assumed command of the Union forces in the Western Theater and rescued the army in Chattanooga. In late November Grant's reinforcements captured the heights around Chattanooga in the battle of Missionary Ridge. The 78th Pennsylvania, as part of Rosecrans's former army, watched the battle for the high ground from their entrenchments in the city. They had helped to secure Tennessee and now knew that a spring offensive would drive the army into Georgia.

In this crisis year, from the eastern campaigns to the western ones, Indiana Countians once again had responded to the nation's needs. Neither they nor President Lincoln knew that the tide had turned. While forthcoming events and battles would require continued sacrifice and commitment, the Union was winning the war and a new nation was emerging.

☆ CHAPTER 5 ☆

IMPACT OF THE WAR ON INDIANA COUNTY

On May 7, 1862, a new political force, the *Indiana Democrat*, burst forth on the scene in Indiana County. Calling for "The Union as it was, the Constitution as it is," James B. Sansom, the editor of the *Indiana Democrat*, launched what became a provocative and volatile career. The present Civil War, he exclaimed, was the work of "fanatical agitation in the North on the question of domestic slavery . . . a sectional party and the development of sectional hate. . . ." In an effort to establish that his party, the Northern Democrats, represented the moderate political attitudes, Sansom declared that "we utterly abhor and detest the twin heresies of secession and abolitionism. . . ."[1]

The appearance of the *Indiana Democrat* marked one of the significant changes that the war brought to Indiana County. Though far away from the battlefields and the citadels of policy making, Indiana County could not escape the war unscathed. The turbulence of war, Indiana Countians soon realized, extended far beyond the battlefield and affected rural communities more than they had anticipated. The issues of wartime brought divisions into the community that had been muted in 1861, and the political atmosphere of Indiana County became especially charged. Moreover, Indiana Countians had to adapt to the inflationary costs of war and the disruption in their economic lives. Certainly, one of the unexpected intrusions into the daily life was the increase in government expenses that demanded more taxes. Indiana Countians, like Americans elsewhere, realized by 1862 that the Civil War was altering the course of their lives.

James B. Sansom became in many ways the symbolic figure of the changes and controversy that came with the war. A thirty-six-year-old father of six when he came to Indiana County, Sansom understood that the newspaper business in the nineteenth century required men to have courage and ambition—and political

69

connections. To operate a newspaper, and thus to survive as a businessman, the editor-publisher required political associations from whom he would receive advertisements, spicy items for his pages, and printing contracts from the local and state government. The editor needed a multiplicity of talents, namely those of writer, fighter (in print and sometimes in the streets), and salesman. He needed to possess a strong ego for he knew the opposition would spare no ink or vocabulary in competing with him. He needed to recognize that the words in his newspaper would attract readers; thus, journalism became an amalgam of credibility and sensationalism. Sansom satisfied all these qualities and came to Indiana County with ten years of experience as editor of the *Fulton County Democrat*.[2]

Sansom probably came to Indiana County at the invitation of the Democratic leaders like Hugh Wier and Silas Clark. Wier, a successful lawyer in Indiana Borough, spoke for the Democratic Party and was its candidate for several offices. Clark, a twenty-eight-year-old lawyer, was a rising star in the Democratic Party. Born in nearby Elderton, Clark graduated from Jefferson College in Cannonsburg, taught school for a while, was admitted to the bar in Indiana County in 1857, and contributed to a newspaper, the *Democratic Messenger*, which lasted for a year.[3] When the paper changed politics from Democratic to independent in solidly Republican Indiana County, the minority party lacked a true editorial voice. Undoubtedly, Wier, Clark, and other Democrats by 1862 thought the time was ripe for a newspaper of their persuasion.

The Democratic Party during the Civil War represented the conservative ideology of that era. Sansom's masthead always read: "The Union as it was, the Constitution as it is." To the Democrats, the Lincoln administration and the war were undermining the Constitution and introducing racial amalgamation. Sansom clearly outlined the Democratic credo in his second issue that appeared on the streets. Charging the Republicans as "political charlatans" who were robbing the treasury, Sansom predicted that a brighter day was dawning for the masses who have been "hood-winked and blinded by specious arguments." The Republicans, he charged, espoused "social and political equality for the white and black races" contrary to the will of God. The Democrats, on the other hand, feared for the workingmen who would lose jobs to emancipated slaves that might migrate north. The Democrats, he assured his readers, did not support slavery, but believed that the institution should remain under the jurisdiction of the states as the Constitution had provided.[4]

Sansom's message altered little in the next few years. He accused the Lincoln administration of political arrests and violation of civil liberties, called the war effort a "reign of terror and fanaticism," and charged the Republicans as being "given over to the rapacity of plunderers and speculators." After Lincoln issued the Emancipation Proclamation in January 1863, Sansom argued that the "war for suppression of the rebellion" had been perverted to "a war for Emancipation . . . an act of gross injustice" to the soldiers. Sansom exhibited little restraint in competing with the Republican newspapers in Indiana County. A newspaper war ensued in Indiana County in 1862 and 1863, and Sansom fired journalistic salvo after salvo at his competition. He accused the *Weekly Register* of "radicalism" and boldly charged that the editor of the *Messenger* was "A LIAR AND A MALICIOUS SLANDERER." Yet, his skin had to be tough for he bore much abuse, too. His principal adversary, August Row, finally called Sansom a "contemptible rebel, who shines and stinks and stinks and shines like a polecat . . . a rebel-editor who spews his filth weekly."[5]

Sansom also came under attack from the nine-month volunteers in the 135th Pennsylvania when they returned to Indiana in May 1863. Recently battle tested at Fredericksburg, these veterans wanted demonstrations of loyalty from the Democrats. They visited several private homes and Sansom's office and required that the Democrats fly an American flag outside their residences.[6] Sansom was living proof that the minority has to compromise to the will of the majority.

The Republican Party had dominated Indiana County's politics since the late 1850s. It had a powerful publicity agent in the *Weekly Register*, edited by the Row brothers, August and George. A third newspaper in Indiana County, *The Messenger*, edited by J. Willis Westlake and Samuel A. Smith, attempted to pursue a nonpartisan course. Only after suffering from Sansom's fiery attacks did *The Messenger* enter the newspaper wars of 1862.[7]

Former Whigs like George Row, Judge Thomas White, A. W. Taylor, and William H. Stewart had built the Republican Party in Indiana County. During the war new leaders emerged like Thomas St. Clair, a thirty-six-year-old physician in 1860, who gained some celebrity as the first surgeon west of the Allegheny Mountains to remove an ovarian tumor.[8]

Spearheading the Republicans in Indiana County was Harry White, fourth and youngest child of Judge Thomas White. Educated at Princeton, he read law and was admitted to the Indiana County bar in 1856. That year he turned twenty-one years old and demonstrated his ambitious nature by organizing the Republican Party in Indiana County. A year older than Silas Clark, the chieftain of the Democratic Party, White commenced a longstanding personal and political rivalry through the creation of the Republican Party. Supportive of Lincoln during the secession crisis White recognized that a military career would enhance his political aspirations. He organized a volunteer company from Brush Valley, and later gained a political appointment from Governor Curtin to be a major in the 67th Pennsylvania Regiment.[9]

White's military service did not mean his withdrawal from politics. He learned that Republicans back in Indiana County planned to nominate him as a candidate for state senator in 1862 and that August Row had publicized White's availability. He wrote his father that he could not obtain a furlough to campaign and that he did not think "it will be good policy to leave my post here." But, in what probably is the most extensive list of a political organization ever revealed, he gave his father the names of friends and political associates throughout Indiana County who would help White's campaign. Harry White continued to monitor the campaign from afar in Annapolis, Maryland. He sent a second letter with additional names of persons who would assist his campaign and suggested that someone write the soldiers in "Jim Porter's Regiment [the 135th Pennsylvania] to vote as well as for Senator as for Congress." Hearing that Hugh Wier was avidly assisting White's opponent, Joseph M. Thompson, White urged his father to do "everything possible . . . to prevent defeat."[10]

White won the election in 1862, but the most surprising aspect of the results was that the Democratic candidate, John L. Dawson from Fayette County, became the district's new congressman. The 1862 elections followed the news of the losses in the battles of Second Bull Run and Antietam, Lincoln's issuance of the First Emancipation Proclamation, and the controversy over the first draft. Across the state, Democrats anticipated that Lincoln's troubles would enable them to gain state and congressional seats. They failed to win control of the Pennsylvania legislature but gained four seats in the lower house, two in the state senate, and four seats in the congressional delegation.[11] In Indiana County, the Democratic total vote climbed a modest five percent. The party carried only Cherry Tree but improved its standing in Armstrong, Brush Valley, Burrell, Center, Green, White, East Wheatfield, and West Wheatfield Townships between twenty-five and seven percent. To some degree the tallies were affected by the absence of men who had entered the military. "We have too many in the army to hope for victory," lamented one Republican. It was still clear that the draft, war results, and emancipation were concerns of Indiana Countians. "There is much discussion among the people who is to blame McClellan or the President for the . . . great slaughter."[12]

Lincoln's Emancipation Proclamation in January 1863 elicited a strong response from the Democrats in Indiana County. At a dinner meeting of two hundred people in Blairsville, the party condemned the president for changing war objectives from preservation of the Union to the emancipation of blacks. With those resolutions the party indicated it would continue to focus on the race issue and emancipation during the political campaigns. The Democrats staged several meetings and parades in Armagh, Blairsville, Cherry Tree, and Indiana in 1863 to arouse support for their gubernatorial candidate, George W. Woodward. They announced their support of the soldiers in the field, but objected to emancipation as a war aim.[13]

The Democrats in Pennsylvania and Indiana County mounted a strong challenge in 1863. Woodward lost the state election to the incumbent governor, Andrew Curtin, by less than 16,000 votes. In Indiana County, the Democratic tally continued to climb. While garnering only 33 percent of the vote, an increase of 7 percent over 1860, the Democratic vote increased from 1,347 to 1,955 votes. By gaining a majority of the votes in Canoe and Cherry Tree townships, and winning nearly forty percent of the vote in Burrell, Pine, Saltsburg, and West Wheatfield, the Democrats demonstrated vitality throughout the county.[14]

As the new General Assembly convened for its 1864 session Indiana County was thrust into the center of state politics. In the state senate the seat held by now-imprisoned Colonel Harry White could determine a balance of power. Without White in the senate, each party controlled thirty-two seats. The situation bore some urgency because under Pennsylvania's constitution no office of lieutenant governor existed, and Governor Curtin bordered on physical and emotional collapse. Curtin had maintained a workaholic pace during his first term in attending to the state responsibilities and assisting President Lincoln in finding troops and support in the Commonwealth. Curtin's black hair by 1864 had turned nearly white, and though he was only forty-eight years old his manner was that of an aged person. Exhausted and attended to by several physicians, Curtin had considered surrendering the governorship in 1863. But President Lincoln needed a strong Republican in Pennsylvania and urged Curtin to run for re-election with the promise of a comfortable ambassadorship in a congenial climate after Curtin finished his term. After the election Curtin became so ill that Lincoln provided a navy cutter to take him to Cuba for rest. Consequently, Pennsylvania needed an interim governor.[15]

The Pennsylvania constitution stipulated that the speaker of the senate was to be the successor to the governor. Between sessions of the legislature the senate traditionally chose an interim speaker to serve in case the governor became incapacitated. In 1864, with Curtin so ill, the circumstances suggested that the interim speaker, John C. Penney of Pittsburgh, a Republican, might assume the governorship. But the Democrats, in the evenly divided senate, envisioned that they might be able to choose the speaker. Each party expected that their candidate would replace the desperately ill Curtin and give their party control of the governor's mansion with all its power and patronage. For two months the state senators argued and stalled in the power struggle. It was obvious that Harry White, incarcerated in Dixie, held the deciding vote.

Attempts by Pennsylvania Republicans and the Lincoln administration to exchange White for some high-ranking Confederate met with no result. With no end to the quandary in sight Republicans in Harrisburg anxiously sought Harry White's resignation. George Getty, in urging Judge Thomas White to obtain his son's resignation, argued that Harry had much to gain by his resignation. "If he makes this sacrifice the country will never forget it", Getty wrote. "I know that public opinion is fast settling down to this point."[16]

From newspapers smuggled into prison Harry White became aware of the deadlock he was causing in the Pennsylvania senate. He wrote his resignation in November 1864, Penney later stated, placed it in the binding of a Bible, and gave it to Dr. William S. Hosack of Pittsburgh who was being exchanged. Hosack, upon his arrival in Pennsylvania, delivered the message to Harry's father, Judge White. But Judge White, hoping to retain Harry's seat for him in the state senate, did not make the letter public until he was convinced that Harry would not be exchanged. He submitted it to the senate on February 1, 1864. Ignoring Democrats' claims that the letter was not genuine, Speaker Penney immediately authorized Indiana County to conduct a special election on February 19 to replace Harry White. Accordingly, on February 19, voters in Indiana County went to the polls to choose either Dr. Thomas St. Clair, the Republican, or James Douglas, the Democrat, as the new state senator. The Republicans demonstrated once again their strength in Indiana County as St. Clair polled 73 percent of the vote. St. Clair hurried to Harrisburg, the Republicans quickly organized the senate and voted 17–16 in favor of Penney as speaker. With Indiana County's assistance, Pennsylvania's constitutional crisis was over.[17]

By September 1864 both parties in Indiana County had prepared for an active presidential campaign. Sansom appealed to Democrats, conservatives, and moderate Republicans to unite behind George B. McClellan, the Democratic candidate and former commander of the Army of the Potomac. Like most election year slogans, the Democratic slogan,"LIBERTY, THE UNION, THE CONSTITUTION, FREE SPEECH, A FREE PRESS & EQUAL RIGHTS," aimed to find the most common denominator. The Republicans in Indiana County countered the Democrats' rhetoric with political fireworks. They called upon veterans whose tour of duty had ended to lead a grand parade of Republicans a few days prior to the presidential election. Indiana County, once again, demonstrated the strength of Republicanism as Lincoln carried 65 percent of the vote.[18]

In an area and a time when the Republican Party had established its dominance, Sansom, Wier, Clark, and other Democrats suffered much frustration. Since 1860 the Democratic Party in Indiana County had increased its strength by 10 percent and showed some popularity in Canoe, Cherry Tree, Conemaugh, Saltsburg, and West Wheatfield townships. But the key political development of this era was the establishment of the Civil War Party System in which the Republican Party saved the Union and freed the slaves. Republicanism became the credo of Indiana Countians and most Northerners until the mid-twentieth century.

J. B. Sansom continued to fight vigorously for the Democratic Party's values in Indiana County. Among the themes upon which he hammered was the economic plight which the Civil War wrought upon the laboring class. Rising prices, he claimed with some truth, had trapped the working people in a vicious inflationary spiral. Every war brings a demand for more food, clothing, and munitions to support an army. The increased demand results in inflationary spirals and the Civil War was no different. From 1860 to 1865, the consumer price index rose nationally by 75 percent.[19] Spiralling food costs crimped the budget of laborers and produced hardships for the ordinary family. The Indiana newspapers alluded to the rising costs from time to time, and regularly reported a "market report."

Chart I

Indiana County Market Prices, 1861–1865

	1861	1865	Percent Change
Farm Products:			
Red Wheat	1.00	2.25	125
White Wheat	1.10	2.30	109
Rye	.45	1.50	233
Corn	.40	1.20	200
Oats	.22	.85	286
Buckwheat	.40	.90	125

	1861	1865	Percent Change
Timothy	1.50	5.00	233
Clover	4.50	15.00	233
Flax	1.10	3.00	173
Consumer Goods:			
Bacon	.12	.22	83
Butter	.14	.40	186
Eggs	.12	.30	150
Flour	6.50	12.00	85
Lard	.10	.25	150
Salt	1.50	4.25	183
Construction Products:			
Pine Boards	1.00	2.50	150
Shingles, Lap	5.25	11.00	110

(Source: *Indiana Weekly Register*, 1861–1865)

The chart shows that many consumer products in Indiana County doubled in price from 1861 to 1865. A pound of butter, for example, rose from 14 cents to 40 cents; a dozen of eggs, 12 cents to 30 cents. That inflationary spiral exceeded the skyrocketing prices that Americans felt in the 1970s.

But, in spite of the hardships Sansom described, the Civil War may have been Indiana County's era of strongest economic growth. In examining the inflationary spiral from the market report, one must remember that Indiana County was predominantly a farming community. Without question the Civil War spurred farm prices and production throughout the North, and the farmers benefitted from the wartime inflation. As wheat prices rose by 125 percent, the grain farmer enjoyed greater profits. Similarly, the rise in dairy prices by 180 percent and the increase in wood products by over 100 percent poured more money into the pockets of the farmers. Indiana County's farmers clearly shared in the economic boom of the Civil War. They cleared more land and the average size of farms increased from 97 to 116 acres. Additionally, more people became farmers; the number of farms increased by 7 percent, 3,389 in 1860 to 3,621 in 1870. County farm values increased 89 percent over the pre-war years and farm tools increased 54 percent in value.[20]

A qualitative change also occurred in Indiana County's agriculture. County farmers shifted from dairy products (butter and cheese declining by over 80 percent) to enjoy the high prices of the grain market. Wheat and corn prices attracted the attention of Indiana

County farmers. Wheat and barley production increased fivefold, and corn production increased by 171 percent. Prior to the war wool production had nearly stabilized. But as the market prices increased and as newspapers reported that factories were working overtime to meet the demand for woolen uniforms, farmers capitalized on the growing demand.[21] Wool production rose by 15 percent. As the soldiers turned to tobacco for relaxation and as tobacco farms in the South were destroyed, Indiana County farmers experimented with that crop, too. By 1870, the county produced only a piddling 230 pounds of tobacco, but obviously some farmers had their eyes on the market prices of tobacco.

Chart II

Indiana County Farm Products

	1860	1870	Percent Change
Grain (bu.):			
Barley	94	589	527
Buckwheat	276,695	71,477	-74
Clover	4,549	0	-100
Corn	241,039	652,263	171
Oats	653,199	986,255	51
Rye	64,970	97,550	50
Wheat	50,867	308,183	506
Dairy (lbs.):			
Butter	1,011,878	110,095	-89
Cheese	53,181	7,874	-85
Other (lbs.):			
Flax	15,117	19,834	31
Maple Sugar	20,806	0	-100
Potatoes	175,060	77,367	-56
Tobacco	0	230	100
Wool	109,569	125,891	15

(Source: *Agriculture of the United States of the Eighth Census; Compendium of the Ninth Census*)

The picture of animal husbandry remained similar to the pre-war years, except for the increase in mules. They had become the "horsepower" behind the plows in the grain fields.

Chart III

Indiana County Animal Husbandry, 1860–1870

	1860	1870	Percent Change
Value	$1,234,306	$2,174,542	76
Number of Animals:			
Horses	9,712	11,586	19
Mules	80	209	161
Milch Cows	12,627	12,061	-4
Oxen	941	241	-74
Other cattle	16,601	13,603	-18
Sheep	39,917	44,054	10
Swine	21,070	17,412	-17

(Source: *Agriculture of the United States of the Eighth Census; Compendium of the Ninth Census*)

Further evidence of the Civil War as being a boom time for Indiana County can be found in the industrial changes that occurred in the county:

Chart IV

Indiana County Manufacturing, 1860–1870

	1860	1870	Percent Change
No. of Operations	137	473	245
No. of Employees	265	1086	310
Capital Investments	$244,635	$ 918,220	275
Annual Production	$340,811	$1,393,408	309

Industry	Yearly Production in Dollars		
Woolen goods	$ 6,716	$ 57,685	759
Furniture	2,400	14,357	498
Wagons	2,820	16,350	480
Tin, metalware	5,600	31,690	466
Lumber, sawed	30,935	169,216	447
Lumber, planed	4,800	23,550	391
Iron casts	7,300	31,823	336
Clothing	6,200	20,100	224
Farm tools	5,500	13,005	136
Saddlers	0	34,156	100
Mining coal	0	98,026	100
Bricks	0	54,651	100

	1860	1870	Percent Change
RR machinery	$ 0	$ 22,920	100
Leather goods	59,658	111,371	87
Flour milling	131,569	90,755	-31
Carpets	2,000	0	-100
Boots, shoes	8,325	0	-100
Cigars	1,250	0	-100
Cooperage	770	0	-100

(Source: *Manufactures of the United States of the Eighth Census; Compendium of the Ninth Census*)

As Chart IV shows the county enjoyed a tremendous growth in manufacturing. The increase in the number of operations and people employed in manufacturing represents a dramatic shift of the labor force to non-agricultural enterprises. The increase in dollars generated from manufacturing during the Civil War decade by 309 percent meant a significant amount of income for the county. The lumber industry, in sawmills and finishing plants, generated the most income for the county. The increase in woolen goods, furniture, wagons, and metalware indicated that Indiana County had linked to outside markets through the railroad that came into Blairsville and Indiana Borough. New industries like brick making and railroad machinery provided new jobs for Indiana Countians. On the other hand, the traditional family shops characteristic of a localized market like boot makers, coopers, and carpet makers were disappearing from main street.

The Civil War also stimulated the industry that came to underlie the county's economy for the next century—coal mining. The industrial boom of the war demanded more coal, and the soft coal industry of western Pennsylvania profited. Coal mining began in Indiana County in the early nineteenth century and reached a peak production in 1838 of 31,000 tons. The 1837–1843 depression upset the national economy and Indiana County coal production dropped to 19,000 tons in 1843. By 1860 the coal business was nearly defunct; according to the 1860 Census of Manufactures, Indiana County was mining no coal. But the war revived the coal industry. By April 1864 coal companies in Indiana County were working overtime to meet the demand for coal. By the end of the decade coal companies in the county employed over one hundred men, two-thirds of which worked in underground mines, and produced 38,082 tons of coal. Nearly $100,000 came into the county from coal mining.[22]

Historians have debated whether the Civil War stimulated or disrupted industrial growth. Charles and Mary Beard argued long ago that the Civil War represented the American Industrial Revolution. Other historians challenged their thesis by arguing that the Civil War either retarded or minimized economic growth. Recent examinations of local studies, such as J. Matthew Gallman's study of Philadelphia during the war, have argued that qualitative as well as quantitative changes occurred, and that the economy bore immediate as well as long-term effects of the Civil War. The evidence unquestionably demonstrates that the Civil War was a boom time for Indiana County's industrial growth. The number of operations increased by over 200 percent, the number of people employed in manufacturing increased over 300 percent, and the annual production increased over 300 percent. Money flowed into Indiana County and job opportunities increased.[23]

Not everyone shared in the wartime prosperity. Wives and families of the soldiers bore the sacrifices of the breadwinner all too quietly. One woman's frustration surfaced in a letter to the *Democrat*. In order to gain a little money while her drafted husband was fighting for the Union, she was sewing for other folks and taking care of children. She claimed it was unfair that "hundreds and thousands of negroes are kept, and fed, and clothed and some them paid by the Government while the wives and children of the drafted men are left to starve."[24]

Women's experiences during the Civil War have suffered from "historical invisibility."[25] In a male-dominated world, they received little attention from the press and public records in the nineteenth century. In the twentieth century, males dominated the historical profession and generally ignored the role and lives of women in the past. Regrettably, too, many of the sources which might offer insights into the life of women have become lost. While we have thousands of letters of the soldiers in the field kept by families back home, the letters of the wife or loved one to the soldier were discarded. Those letters that would give us the picture of life at home, the loneliness of a spouse, or the sacrifices of a family have become lost to history. Necessarily, then, we have to depend on male sources which offer us only selective and partial visions of the life of the women and families.

Certainly, as we examine these sources we can see that the overriding concern of the husband who either volunteered or was drafted was the economic security of his family. Colonel Richard White sent money home regularly to care for his family's well-being. Interestingly enough, he wired the money not directly to his wife, Kate, but to his father. This evidence provides us another insight into a male-dominated world where the male assumed that the financial affairs of the family was beyond the place or capacity of the woman. William Penn Oberlin of the 148th Pennsylvania, on the other hand, sent money directly to his wife, Annie. His April 17, 1863, letter reports of his sending $30 in greenbacks the previous day and $40 with this letter. He continued to send money and wrote that he was "fully aware that you should have money, and that all goods are high in price." John Compton, who enlisted to avoid the draft in March 1865, received a bounty of $550 and he wrote his wife to make certain the money had been deposited in an Indiana bank. William Coulter, as provost marshal for the 21st Draft District, reported that he was compelled to give furloughs to draftees in order for them to attend to their wives and families before they entered military service.[26]

Disabled and impoverished parents depended upon their sons to send them money from the battlefields. George R. Walker, a volunteer in Company B, 61st Pennsylvania, regularly sent a check home to his parents in Rayne Township. Wounded and dying on the battlefield at Spotsylvania Courthouse in May 1864, he instructed that his watch and all money be forwarded to his mother. Samuel Carbaugh, a volunteer in Porter's company in the 40th Pennsylvania, regularly sent a portion of his paycheck to his dependent parents. When the parents rented a farm, Carbaugh promised to send them money to purchase a team of oxen. After the battle of Antietam, Carbaugh lost his patience with his parents' continual requests for money. "I did not enlist for the purpose of making money," he wrote,

> but for the defense of our country and you know we have hard living here with nothing but Government rations and we need a little money to spend for little things that is a great help to a person when they are not well or on a hard march. And if I had a rich father that I could fall back on if I would get sick and want to come home it would be far different from what it is for if I should want to come home and had no money with me it would be hard to do so. Still I am willing to help you as far as I am able. . . .

John Marlin in the 78th Pennsylvania received a request from a grandfather who wished that Marlin would speak to a grandson in Marlin's company about sending money home. "The old man says that he took care of him when he was a child," Marlin's brother wrote, "and it would be nothing but right for the boy to help him a little when he stands in need of it."[27]

Like many communities throughout the nation, Indiana Countians were sensitive to the needs of the families left behind as the soldiers went to war. The county government created a relief fund to assist soldiers' families and by 1863 had assessed $12,555 from taxes and collected $202 in donations. Because most citizens paid their taxes towards the end of the year, the county had been able to award only $5,199 when the treasurer filed his end-of-the-year report. The following year the treasurer reported $14,603.92 assessed, collected, or donated for the relief fund. Major Harry White showed political acumen as well as humanitarian concerns by donating $350. Unfortunately, laggard taxpayers failed to meet their civic obligations and the county government could dispense only $5,000 to the soldiers' families. Regrettably the loss of county records, either through fire or lack of care, prevents a thorough examination of the relief fund and the dispensation of its funds. We cannot determine how many families received the funds or the amount they received.[28]

Whether they qualified for relief funds or not, the women still had to manage households, small businesses, and farms. Invariably they received letters from their husbands giving instructions or counsel. John Compton, for example, instructed his wife to hire neighbors to cut wood and that she attend "to the bees when they get the worms & keep them raised up on blocks & so the worms don't build nest under them." Yet, the advice and love went both ways. Daughter Sarah Ann, writing for mother, advised Lieutenant John Marlin of the 78th Pennsylvania that a carrot would cure his reported malady. Then concerned that perhaps father might not recognize a carrot she described it as a "garden vegetable and looks something like parsnip of a deep yellow color." From their farm near Penn Run, Pennsylvania Catherine Fair reported to her husband in the spring of 1865 of the birthing of the livestock, the ploughing which the hired hand had done, and the lush blossoms of the pear trees and clover. Knowing that her husband was under the stress of war, she hoped to allay his worries about affairs back home; her letter implied that the farm was operating well.[29]

The separation from home deeply affected the soldiers in the field. Their letters are riddled with symptoms of homesickness. The wives, also, felt the emotional sacrifices. Daughter Sarah Ann alluded to the emotional distress mother was having when she informed Father John Marlin that "mother does not want you to reenlist but she wants you to come home as soon as possible it is just nine months tomorrow to your time will be out." While attempting to suggest to her husband that the family was secure, Catherine Fair could not entirely hide the loneliness and loss caused by the separation. In a very loving letter expressing wishes that her husband was home, she ended with the hope that "there will not [be] many nights elapse till we meet."[30]

Mrs. Fair enjoyed a happy ending to the war. Her husband returned home safe and sound. For thousands of other women, the war had a tragic end. Their husbands were killed and they were left alone and penniless. Congress addressed the problem of the handi-capped veteran and the impoverished widow with a series of pension acts. Congress enacted an initial Civil War pension in 1862 and later broadened the scope of federal responsibilities to enhance the lives of Civil War veterans, widows, and families. By 1893 forty per-cent of the federal budget was earmarked for pensions, a substantial portion of which went to Civil War widows. A woman could receive a pension if she could prove that her husband died from a wound and disease stemming from his military service. The pension which she received ranged between $8 and $30 a month. If the widow received the maximum amount her yearly income was $360 which was equiva-lent to the average yearly wage for a non-farm worker in 1865. Pen-sions bills enacted in 1868 and 1886 increased the minimum monthly allowance to $12 and gave widows a $2 monthly pension for each dependent child.[31]

Fortunately, dependent women in Indiana County shared in this federal program. By 1883, thirty-one percent (129) of the Civil War pensioners in Indiana County were women. Several received pensions between $10 and $17 per month, but most received the minimum $8 per month or $96 per year. For the county, that repre-sented at least $12,384 coming into the economy yearly. While the pensions in no way compensated for the loss of life and love that each woman sacrificed, at least the women had an economic safety net insuring them from an impoverished life. Among the women who received a pension was Samuel Carbaugh's mother. She ap-plied for a pension in 1868 and was awarded an $8 per month pension retroactive to May 1, 1863. In death as in life Samuel Carbaugh had provided for his parents' well-being.[32]

Certainly one of the tragic impacts of war on a community is the number of men who die. When we think of World War I we are reminded of the generation of British and French soldiers who were lost in that war. As we think of American wars many of us remem-ber the effect that the Vietnam deaths had on our society. Nightly television news with the body bags and the attrition rate perme-ated America with a sense of death. The collection of the 55,000 names on the Vietnam Memorial renders a graphic display that tears at our heart.

Historians have shown us the wide swath that the Grim Reaper cut on a national scale from the Civil War.[33] As the statistics demon-strate, the losses in the Civil War exceeded American deaths in any other war. American society, 1861–1865, just as in the Vietnam era, was deeply affected by the casualties. When we narrow the picture to the local level we see more clearly and feel more deeply the impact that the deaths had on the community. Using newspaper reports,

pension applications, and J. F. Stewart's roster of Civil War partici-
pants in his 1918 county history, I compiled a list of Indiana County
soldiers who lost their lives during the Civil War. As the table below
shows 414 Indiana Countians lost their lives in the Civil War. The
death rate for Indiana Countians, ages 15–45, presumably the age
group for soldiers, was 6 percent, which is comparable to the Northern soldiers' death rate nationally.

Deaths of Indiana County Civil War Soldiers

135 killed in action
88 from wounds
23 died in prison
<u>168</u> disease, accident, missing in action

414 total

We frequently overlook the non-action deaths that may occur in
war. In these statistics are the cases of Theodore Pardee of the 84th
Pennsylvania who drowned in the Potomac River at Hancock, Maryland and William Spencer, 105th Pennsylvania, who died in a railroad accident. The data demonstrates the ravages of typhoid fever,
dysentery, and diphtheria on the Civil War army. Additionally, the
number of soldiers dying from wounds reminds us of the primitive
medical and sanitary conditions of the Civil War. Surely, A. J. Bolar,
when he refused to have his legs amputated, may have calculated
the odds of dying as a result of the surgeon's knife.

A second way to demonstrate the impact of the Civil War on
Indiana County is to compare the losses of that war with other
wars and the community's population.

Indiana County Military Deaths[34]

	Total	Per 10,000 Population
Civil War	414	122.0
World War II	322	40.3
Korean War	14	1.82
Vietnam War	25	3.32

This data underscores the pain and agony that the community felt
as it received news of deaths in the field and saw amputees and
wounded return home.

Military psychologists recently have called attention to the
post-traumatic stress disorder. As one historian has suggested

certainly Civil War veterans just as Vietnam veterans suffered a variety of emotional problems after the war. One wonders how vigorous, young men in a predominantly agricultural community, such as Indiana County, adapted to the loss of an arm and leg. One's income and livelihood in most instances depended upon brute strength and physical labor. Certainly an amputee may have felt a loss of masculinity and wondered about his financial well-being. Surely a veteran who had lost an arm or a leg fell into the pits of deep depression. Consider, for example, Bill Hamilton of the 40th Pennsylvania. A twenty-year-old farm boy in South Mahoning Township in 1860, he enlisted in 1862 in Company I. He survived the ferocious fighting which the 40th Pennsylvania weathered until the battle of Spotsylvania. There he was shot and he came home with one leg amputated. A few years after the war Hamilton limped into the forests to hunt game. He returned to his sweetheart's home, sat on the porch steps, leaned on the muzzle of the gun with his chin, knocked the hammer of the weapon, and died with a gunshot blast to the head. At the time people assumed that he had died from an accident. Perhaps so; perhaps not. Today we might suspect that Bill Hamilton was so depressed from having to face life with a severe disability that he committed suicide.[35]

As Bill Hamilton's life and death suggest, our histories are not divided into perforated lines. Events and experiences affect us for the rest of our lives. Similarly the Civil War's impact on Indiana County, whether it be in politics or economics, taxes or death, was felt for many years after Appomattox.

☆ CHAPTER 6 ☆

THE FINAL STRUGGLES

Soldiering did not turn out as Harry White had expected. Rather than finding glory, perhaps even a generalship, and advancing his political fortune, perhaps even a candidacy for the governor's mansion, White found himself on January 12, 1864, staring at four walls in a dirt floor cellar prison in North Carolina. Placed in solitary confinement he reflected upon his previous year and the hopelessness of his situation: "The contrast is palpable and striking . . . I had started upon a career of public life with hope and promise of, at least, usefulness and respectability . . . Today I have confinement, weary, irksome feelings and little hope for myself for the future."[1]

Harry White's plight was one of the many tragic, if heroic, situations which the Indiana County soldier faced in the final struggles of the nation's Civil War. While he contemplated his fate and languished in the depths of depression (April 28, 1864: "The gloomy feelings of this day have been to me oppressive, almost beyond endurance." May 7, 1964: "I have felt a little gloomy during the day. I find it difficult to read much these days."), the Union army launched the final offensive that would take it to the eventual defeat of the rebels. Other Indiana Countians played a significant role in those final struggles, and some paid the ultimate sacrifice for the Union.

The spring campaigns of 1864 witnessed a new vigor in the Union army. General U. S. Grant assumed command of all the Union armies and brought to the Union war effort an understanding of grand strategy which all other generals—Union and Confederate— lacked. Additionally, Grant demonstrated a tenacity and single-mindedness that the Union army badly needed. He coordinated a total offensive of western and eastern armies for 1864–65 and refused to relax the attack. Though resulting in a merciless and bloody war, Grant's strategy was necessary to bring the Civil War to a close.

One of Grant's assignment went to General Ben Butler with his Army of the James. Butler's task was to cut the Richmond and Petersburg Railroad and threaten Richmond from the south. Butler received reinforcements from coastal forces to assist in this campaign. After spending most of the war on the quiet North Carolina coast, Richard White's 55th Pennsylvania was one of the regiments called in to aid Butler. Butler's army skirmished with Confederates daily as it moved up the James River. On May 16, under cover of heavy fog the rebels attacked the extreme left of the Union line which the 55th anchored. Outflanked and nearly surrounded, Colonel White selected Companies C, D, and F to charge against the advancing rebels. This maneuver failed to stall the rebels who swarmed over the 55th's line and captured many of the men, including Colonel White.[2] Now Judge Thomas White had two sons, Richard and Harry, imprisoned in Confederate cells.

As Butler's army penetrated southern Virginia, the Army of the Potomac maneuvered into the heartland of the Old Dominion. Grant's mission for the Army of the Potomac was to pursue and destroy Robert E. Lee's army. "Wherever Lee goes," Grant ordered General George Meade, commander of the Army of the Potomac, "there you will go also." On May 3–4, 1864, the Army of the Potomac moved out of its encampment at Brandy Station, crossed the Rapidan, and headed south. Grant and Meade hoped to find Lee and force him into a battle. The two armies found each other in the Wilderness.

The Wilderness was that immense forest east of Fredericksburg which had been the site of the battle of Chancellorsville. Now exactly a year later the two armies found themselves positioned for battle again in familiar territory. Thick with tangled growth of oak and pines, the Wilderness offered no grand clearings for line assaults. The dense forest nullified long- range artillery fire and hindered the movement of large units. The trees and the bushes obscured battlefield alignments, and soldiers could not see clearly one hundred feet ahead of themselves. Grant initially had no intention of engaging Lee in this massive wilderness, but chance encounters brought the two armies into a bloody collision.[3]

On the morning of May 5, the V Corps, commanded by General Gouverneur Warren, marched south along the Germanna Plank Road through the forests. At the head of the march was the Pennsylvania Reserve Division, commanded by Brigadier General Samuel W. Crawford, and including the Indiana Countians in the 40th and 41th Regiments. The Pennsylvanians were less than enthusiastic about this advance than they had been about earlier battles. They were war weary, their ranks were depleted, and they had only twenty-seven days left on their three-year enlistment. They did not welcome one more chance of getting wounded or killed; their hope now was to survive the last days of their duty unscathed. They had fought at Gaines Mill, Malvern Hill, South Mountain, and Gettysburg; they needed no other battle ribbon to honor their regimental colors. As they marched deeper and deeper into the forests with the foreboding shadows enveloping them, the Pennsylvanians suspected that destiny had marked them for one more fight with "Bobby Lee."

As the center of the V Corps came to the intersection of the Germanna Plank Road and the Orange-Fredericksburg Turnpike it stumbled upon Confederates advancing up the turnpike from the west. The two armies quickly traded fire and Warren wheeled his forces into action facing westward into the forests. The battle of the Wilderness had begun.

Crawford's Pennsylvanians held the southernmost point on the line at the Chewning farm. For several hours they exchanged fire with the rebels, but by 11:30 a.m. activity ceased. Crawford worried that the rebels might take the Orange Plank Road just to the edge of his troops and circle around his line. Additionally the Pennsylvanians were too far from the other Union divisions now into severe combat. Fearful that a gap might appear in the Union line, the corps commander ordered Crawford to pull his men back and connect more closely with other Union divisions. Crawford ordered the regiments to move back, but in the thick forest growth the Pennsylvanians became disoriented. Realizing that they had lost contact with the Union line they picked up the pace looking for signs of the other regiments. Running through the small oaks and pines the 40th Pennsylvania, including Colonel Dan Porter, Captain Hannibal Sloan, and the Indiana volunteers, who were leading the way, rushed into a small clearing only to find a rebel line blocking their escape path. They pulled their rifles into firing position and with suicidal-like screams charged into the Confederate ranks. The stunned Confederates momentarily gave way and the Pennsylvanians broke through the lines. But, the rebels recovered their positions and captured some of the Pennsylvanians running through the gap. James L. O'Neal of the Indiana Guard had been wounded in nearly every battle and recovered; this time his luck ran out. The rebels captured him and he was never heard from again. By early afternoon the remaining elements of the Pennsylvania Reserve gathered on the Union line.[4]

Jacob Creps's Company A in the 61st Pennsylvania also added another battle ribbon to their regimental colors. The 61st Pennsylvania had used the winter lull to bring the regiment up to full

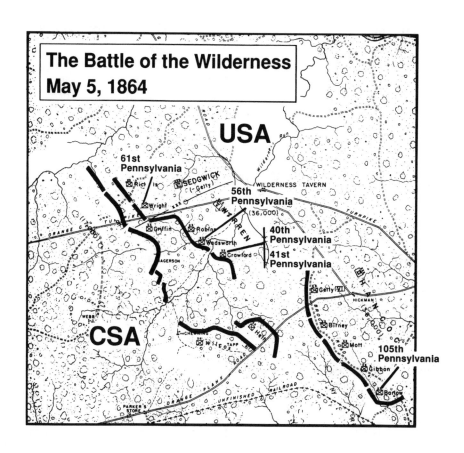

The Battle of the Wilderness
May 5, 1864

strength. Creps and fourteen men returned to Indiana County on a recruiting furlough and met with some success. John Titterington, for example, who had previously served in the 135th (the nine-month regiment) joined his son Aaron, and enlisted in Creps's company February 25, 1864. Now on May 5, the 61st Pennsylvania spearheaded the charge up the Orange Courthouse Turnpike and was the first of the VI Corps to receive fire. The 61st Pennsylvania and its sister regiments anchored the right of the Union line for the remainder of the afternoon.[5] Union and Confederate units charged and countercharged through the heavy forests all afternoon. One of Indiana County's veterans later remembered this battle as[6]

> one volley after another; next, it was one roar, yes, a mighty roar of tens of thousands of muskets. . . Of all the infantry engagements of the war this was no doubt the greatest, the most terrific. There was something grand about it.

The soldiers of the 61st fired over 100 rounds apiece and their rifles at times were too hot to hold. The trees caught fire, and soon acrid smoke and flames added to the intense heat of this hellish day. The rebels assaulted the 61st at one time through a thicket, but Captain Creps ordered the men to hold their fire until the Confederates were clearly through the line of trees. Then Creps led a countercharge and Company A drove the rebels back half a mile into the forests. It was not until 10 p.m. that rifle fire along this line subsided.[7]

Soldiers on either side slept little that night as the rebels launched an attack at 4:30 a.m. on May 6. Rebel artillery rained grapeshot on Union positions killing Lieutenant Frank M. Brown, one of the original enlistees from Indiana County. For five hours the battle raged, assaults met with counterassaults, and the lines became confused. Many soldiers found themselves amidst the enemy and were captured. John Titterington, who had just enlisted in February, was among these unfortunate captives. He eventually ended up at the notorious Confederate prison, Andersonville, where his health was severely impaired. His son, Aaron, became sick some weeks later at Cold Harbor, was taken by ambulance to a hospital, and presumably died. Besides a father and son relationship, the 61st also had twenty-two sets of brothers. Isaac and Lemuel Brady were among these, and Isaac was killed on May 6.[8]

As the battle ensued, Hancock's II Corps joined the Union line. This corps contained the 105th, known as the "Wildcat Regiment", and the 148th Regiment both which had Indiana County volunteers. In the "Wildcat Regiment" Companies F and K had originated in northern Indiana County, but Company I also included Matthias Manner and other Indiana volunteers.

The Wilderness was not a new area to the 105th. When the regiment arrived in the area on May 4, the Pennsylvanians encamped on the same ground where only a year before they had fought in the battle of Chancellorsville. They were able to trace the shallow graves of their comrades who had died in that battle. Colonel Craig and several of the men found the partially uncovered grave of Captain Robert Kirk from Canoe Township in Indiana County. "We identified his remains," Colonel Craig reported, "by a peculiar mark on his shoulder-straps, one of which still adhered to his bones."[9]

About 2 p.m. the II Corps swung into line on the most southern extremity of the Union line facing southwest. This maneuver placed the 105th in one of the most hotly-contested areas of the battle. At 4 p.m. the 105th relieved the 63rd Pennsylvania on the front lines and for four hours traded fire with the Confederates. The Wilderness battle was the fiercest battle the 105th fought during the entire war. "There was scarcely a minute that some one would not come to me and say, 'Colonel, I am wounded,'" reported the regimental commander, "while many could not do so their fate being instantly sealed."[10] At Fair Oaks in 1862 when fifty-three men fell, the 105th believed it had been decimated; at the Wilderness, the 105th lost fifty-six men killed, missing or wounded.[11] Among its killed was Matthias Manner.

The Blairsville soldiers in the 56th Pennsylvania found themselves in the midst of the battle, too. As part of Wadsworth 4th Division (also in V Corps), on May 5 and 6 they valiantly attempted to plug holes in a sagging Union line.[12]

After two days (May 5–6) of slugging it out with no apparent decision, the battle weary armies had no spirit for a continuation of the contest for a third day. Both armies bled badly; the Union army sustained 17,500 casualties, the Confederates, 10,000. Nearby Fredericksburg became the hospital zone for the Union army and wagonloads of wounded and maimed soldiers streamed for the tiny village. One Indiana Countian who served in the ambulance corps recalled that he spent ten consecutive days after the battle carrying the wounded to Fredericksburg. The horses, he recalled, were not unhitched and kept with nose bags filled with feed. After a few days the horses collapsed from exhaustion.[13]

With the bloody battle ending in a stalemate, the Union soldiers anticipated a retreat northward, but Grant demonstrated his mettle and ordered the army to march southward. He wanted to take the vital crossroads at Spotsylvania, a dozen miles away which Lee would have to defend or surrender access to Richmond. Lee decided to obstruct the Union advance and the battle for Spotsylvania ensued.

The contest for Spotsylvania lasted for ten days, May 9–19, with the two armies on a north-south axis. Like the battle of the Wilderness only a few days before, Spotsylvania featured heavy fighting, particularly on a Confederate salient, the "bloody angle." Nearly all regiments in the Union army fought in the see-saw battle, and again Indiana Countians found themselves in the midst of a historic affair.

Though its enlistment time was winding down, the Pennsylvania Reserve did not flinch from battle. In the heat of the battle on May 10 and 12, the Pennsylvania Reserve regiments assaulted the center of the Confederate line. Indiana Countians continued to fall as the 40th Pennsylvania lost over 140 men. Among those lost was Lieutenant Archibald Stewart who had been one of the original young enthusiasts in April 1861 that eagerly volunteered for the Indiana Guard. He had gone through the war unscathed but this time Lady Luck abandoned him. He received a gunshot wound in his right forearm, and by the time he attained proper medical treatment gangrene had set in. He died within a few days as one of the Pennsylvania Reserves' last casualties.[14]

On May 8 Creps's Company A in the 61st was part of an end-of-the-day assault on Confederate positions. As they probed forward into the settling twilight, the 61st stumbled upon a hidden Confederate line. A Confederate officer quickly claimed the 61st's battle flag and ordered the regiment to surrender. But the 61st's color sergeant refused to give up the colors and both sides began to fire their weapons. The initial shots were followed by a melee in which two armies merged into hand-to-hand combat. With darkness coming on, the 61st drove off the battered rebels.[15] Years later one of the Indiana County veterans remembered this engagement:[16]

> Samuel Barnett had a tussle with a large officer, capturing him; George Weaver lost a finger; James H. Stewart received a skull wound from the butt of a gun; a Johnny put the muzzle of a gun to John E. Allison's breast, but the gun did not discharge and in turn Allison shot the Johnny; a Johnny ordered me to surrender and I said, "You will or I will rip you open with my knife!" and the Johnny said, "O, don't! don't! I will surrender. Sergeant Lemuel Brady ordered one to surrender and another one shot the Sergeant dead by my side, and P. S. Justice shot the one that shot Sergeant Brady; J. H. Work captured one and the second one, a large man broke loose from him. They finally retreated, leaving their colors in front of the 61st Regiment.

Sergeant Brady was one of the brother sets in the 61st Pennsylvania and it was his brother that had died a few days earlier in the

Wilderness. Another Indiana Countian, young George R. Walker, who had enlisted in Company B at Pittsburgh in August 1861, also was mortally wounded at Spotsylvania.[17]

Creps's Indiana Countians in Company A, 61st Pennsylvania, continued to be in the midst of ferocious fighting as this regiment took its heaviest toll since Fair Oaks in 1862. On May 12, Creps's command joined the assault on the west side of the Confederate salient. At this particular part of the salient, the so-called "bloody angle," occurred some of the hardest fighting of the war. Bruce Catton in his memorable work, *A Stillness at Appomattox,* called it the "darkest cockpit" of the war.[18] The 61st was one of the regiments which tried to dislodge the Confederates' tenacious hold on the "bloody angle." Only sixty feet apart the battle-weary, battle-crazed armies poured murderous fire into one another. Blood flowed in rivulets, and bodies piled up as the fighting went on all day. No one seemed to know how, or to want, to end it. One of the Indiana Countians in the 61st wounded in this engagement remembered this day many years later. "While the war lasted I had no further desire for any more such experience," he wrote. "No money could hire me to go into another such a battle."[19]

To the right of the 61st a Union artillery battery fired at point-blank range into the Confederates. But rebel sharpshooters hunkered behind a massive white oak tree and picked off the Union cannoneers one by one. With his ranks decimated the artillery officer ran to the 61st hollering for assistance. Five Indiana Countians—Sergeant B. F. Rowland, Calvin Work, Martin Moot, Daniel H. Bee, and John Stewart—rushed to man the cannons. Soon the cannons were blazing again into the Confederates, but the reinforcements came under blistering rifle fire from the rebels behind the oak tree. Years later Stewart remembered that event:[20]

> The last I saw of [Corporal Calvin] Work he was on one foot and knee firing, with nothing to protect him in front. Sergeant [Benjamin F.] Rowland lay between the lines cut up with bullets. Rebel fire swept the battery and Martin Moot was killed.

As a result of his wounds Stewart had to have his arm amputated. Only Bee escaped unscathed. Some riflemen in the 61st focused their fire on the sharpshooters behind the white oak and eventually drove them off. But the cannons remained silent the rest of the day; no one wanted to place themselves in that death trap again. The mighty oak was so splintered by rifle fire that shortly after midnight it came crashing down and crushed some of the rebels in their trenches.[21]

The heavy fighting at the Wilderness and Spotsylvania decimated the ranks of the 61st. Its combined losses in both battles showed 51 killed, 215 wounded, and 24 missing in action.[22] Orlando E. Ellis, another one of the brother sets in Company A, retained vivid memories and physical evidence of Spotsylvania. Captured at Fredericksburg in 1863 with a broken arm, Confederate surgeons administered to needs but jocularly promised that "if I ever came back, they would take my arm off close up to the shoulder... at the battle of Spotsylvania I lost my arm and their word came true...."[23] John C. Johnston, a sixteen-year-old 1864 enlistee in Company A also paid a heavy price for his patriotism at Spotsylvania. "A piece of shell struck me in the face," he recounted many years later,[24]

> tore off my left cheek and broke my cheek bone and cut off part of my left ear. Lt. Price and two members of the company examined me and pronounced me dead. In the evening Captain Creps sent a detail of four men with the order to get the body and bury it and mark the grave. In cutting off my equipments and preparing the body for burial they noticed life. They poured water on my face which revived me. I was taken to the field hospital and the surgeon at first refused to dress the wound, saying I would be dead in a few minutes. I told him that he was mistaken and he finally dressed the wounded.

Johnston remained in the army until Lee's surrender.

The Wildcat Regiment, the 105th, as part of Hancock's II Corps fought in the thick of the battle between May 9–13. In several charges and countercharges they acquitted themselves well and captured several Confederate standards. The regiment continued the march with the Army of the Potomac to Petersburg. In early September 1864 enlistments for the original three-year volunteers expired, and the 105th combined with the 63rd Pennsylvania in the siege lines at Petersburg. In late March 1865 the regiment participated in the breakthrough in Confederate lines and the final chase of Lee's army. Their regimental colors at the end of the war included ribbons from every major battle in the East and the 105th Pennsylvania was included in the list of the "three hundred fighting regiments" of the Union army.[25]

The 148th Pennsylvania, which included a small contingent of Indiana Countians in Company E, suffered 301 casualties at Spotsylvania, marking that regiment as the unit which suffered the most in this battle. The most serious casualties in Company E included Second Lieutenant James M. Sutton who suffered a leg wound and had to have it amputated, and David Luckhart who was mortally wounded. Its engagements started on May 10, when the regiment with Barlow's Division circled around on the left side of the Confederate line. They enjoyed some success in breaking through rebel entrenchments but were left hanging when Confederates counterattacked and other Union forces pulled back. Finding

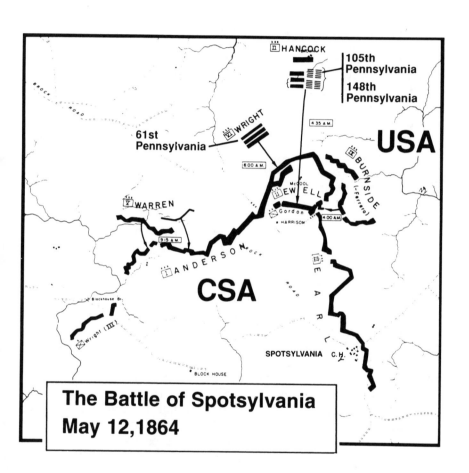

The Battle of Spotsylvania
May 12,1864

themselves nearly encircled the regiment quickly retreated and regained Union lines. The engagement took a heavy toll on the 148th; the unit had 18 men killed, 138 wounded, and 12 were missing.[26]

Two days later the 148th moved to the other side of the Union line to assist in an attack on the Confederates' "bloody angle." The Union mass overcame a stubborn rebel resistance, broke through the salient, and the 148th Pennsylvania received the surrender of the principal Confederate defenders.[27]

Despite the punishment which each army received, neither Grant nor Lee relented. Grant advanced his army farther southward eventually reaching Petersburg on June 15 just south of Richmond. Along the way Lee contested the Union army and vicious battles broke out.

One of these engagements occurred at Bethesda Church which was the last battle for the Pennsylvania Reserves. On May 30, 1864, the advancing Reserves were nearly engulfed by rebel cavalry. The Pennsylvanians quickly piled up rails, logs, and earth as a defensive line. They withstood three rebel charges, then charged themselves from their entrenchments and captured seventy prisoners. On this last day of battle, the Pennsylvanians left the battlefield victorious and the enemy in scattered disarray. The next morning, Tuesday, May 31, their enlistment ended and they were relieved from the front lines.[28]

The Pennsylvania Reserves reached Harrisburg on June 6 where a festive atmosphere welcomed them home. All the stores were closed, the streets were festooned with banners and ribbons, crowds cheered as they marched through the streets, and Governor Curtin extolled their service, sacrifices, and accomplishments.[29] Without question the regiments in the Pennsylvania Reserves compiled an exemplary record. They had participated in every major campaign in the eastern campaigns. Six of the thirteen regiments are included in the celebrated "three hundred fighting regiments" of the Civil War. The 40th Pennsylvania, which included three companies from Indiana County, suffered the heaviest losses of any regiment in the Pennsylvania Reserves, and its 16.6 percent of killed-in-action ranked it eighth of the Union regiments with the highest losses.[30]

From Harrisburg the soldiers took the trains and wagon roads to their homes. Company B, from the old Indiana Guard under the command of Captain Hannibal Sloan, arrived on the noon train on June 15, 1864, in Indiana. They received cheers, welcoming speeches, and dinner at Benford's Hotel. They had left Indiana with a full company in 1861 but returned with only twenty-seven men. Altogether they had twenty-six killed in action.[31]

The 61st Pennsylvania was another regiment whose ranks had dwindled. As it moved with the army southward, the regiment included only 200 men. But it fought in the hard battle at Cold Harbor. There Lieutenant Isaac Price of Indiana County was wounded and when ordered to the rear for medical assistance bravely cried that "he did not want to 'leave the boys.'"[32] Like units in the Pennsylvania Reserve the 61st had fought in some of the toughest battles of the war.

In early July the 61st was reassigned to Washington, D.C. There it took part in the defense of Washington on July 12 at Fort Stevens against a raid by Jubal Early's rebel forces. In Creps's company two brothers, Aseph and John Ellis, had a third brother Horace A. Ellis, who had enlisted in the 7th Wisconsin and was in the hospital in Washington. Horace left the hospital to join his brothers in the defense of Fort Stevens, but when the fighting was done, brother John had been killed. Other losses in Company A were Philip Bowen and Alexander Moore who were mortally wounded. William L. Buchanan lost an arm, and Daniel Bee, who had defended the cannon in the Wilderness and escaped unscathed, lost his gamble with the fates of war. He was wounded in the leg and had to have it amputated.[33]

In August the 61st was assigned to General Phil Sheridan's command in the Shenandoah. There the enlistment time of three years ended for Captain Creps and many Indiana Countians. Yet, they could not escape their final day without a skirmish. Again the regiment was nicked and Lieutenant Isaac Price of Company A was mortally wounded. For Creps and the original members of the 61st that was their final battle. They mustered out and arrived in Indiana County on September 11, 1864. Their service had taken them into the thick of the eastern campaigns and with a regiment that suffered the loss of more officers than any other regiment in the Union army.[34]

Others who completed their three-year tour of duty were members of the 78th Pennsylvania. They have fought at Stones River and Chickamauga and in 1864 joined Sherman's march on Atlanta. By November 4, 1864, the original members of the regiment completed their tenure and they mustered out.[35]

While some Indiana Countians fought in the final struggles against the Confederacy and mustered out in 1864–1865, others languished in Confederate prisons. Among these was Eleaser E. Allen who had not escaped the final battle of the Pennsylvania Reserves with good fortune. He had the misfortune of being captured late in the afternoon, 4:00 p.m., of the last day of service of the Pennsylvania Reserves. Allen had joined Company I, 40th Pennsylvania, when he was only eighteen years old and needed his parents' consent. By late June 1864 his captors took him to the dreaded compounds of the Andersonville Prison. "The sight that met our gaze on entering the pen was sufficient to make a man (or rather a boy) think seriously for a moment," he later remembered. "At least many of the prisoners continued there had been in the pen since the preceding March and nothing but skeletons burned with the sun, hair long and all matted with the pine or pitch smoke and filthy in the extreme." On his first night he witnessed a gang of prisoners raiding other prisoners' supplies of food and quickly understood why. The rations were generally corn bread, the size of a brick, which was to last for twenty-four hours. Sometimes the prisoners "received a piece of bacon the size of a man's thumb, or a pint of greasy water and half a dozen beans on the float." By these latter days of the war, prisoner exchanges were infrequent and Allen, like many others, endured the travails of Andersonville until the end of the war. Yet, he remembered that "the mind of man never rests and in Andersonville we were always scheming escape. Tunnels were in abundance. . . ."[36]

Others who languished in Andersonville were members of the 103rd Pennsylvania. John Stuchell, the original organizer of Company G who recruited heavily in Indiana County, resigned from the army in 1863. James Morrow, his co-recruiter, became captain in 1864. The 103rd was reassigned to duty in coastal North Carolina where they controlled the tidewater rivers. On April 17, 1864, their Plymouth garrison on the Roanoke River came under attack. Company G, serving on the picket line, withstood the initial Confederate attacks. Soon the Union garrison was surrounded and after four days of fighting had to capitulate. Morrow and some officers were paroled but the enlisted men soon found themselves in Andersonville Prison.[37]

Conditions seemed to be little better in the prison at Salisbury, North Carolina. One Indiana Countian remembered that the men were arranged in squads of one hundred men and that "one man did not dare leave his comrades and go into another squad or he would be pounced upon and his grub taken from him, so much like animals had the men become from starvation. . . ."[38]

Others like Colonel Richard White and the soldiers in the 55th Pennsylvania, after a few months of incarceration, were among the lucky ones who were exchanged. Suffering from poor health White was exchanged on August 3, 1864, at Charleston, S.C. He then had to face court-martial indictments of stealing bounty money from his men. After an exhausting trial in which he gained acquittal, White returned to his command. But the regimental surgeon examined him and found the thirty-nine-year-old White to be suffering from angina pectoris, a disease regarded as fatal. The surgeon told White: "We are about to enter into an active campaign and you had better go home to die." White accepted the advice of the surgeon, retired from military service, arrived home in Indiana on March 31, 1865, and died of a heart attack two weeks later on April 14, 1865. At that time his wife, Katherine, was pregnant and would deliver her fourth child on October 21, 1865.[39]

Brother Harry, on the other hand, remained trapped in Confederate prisons. After sixteen months in prison, solitary confinement and abuse had taken its toll on his morale. He confessed, "If it is to continue much longer I could pray for any kind of relief if death itself. I will not, however, give way to those feelings of despondency which come to me so often." Like the prisoners in Andersonville, White contemplated and successfully escaped several times. At one time he was free for twenty-nine days, living with Unionists and blacks in the mountains of South Carolina and Tennessee before Confederate captors and bloodhounds tracked him down. In late September 1864 the two armies agreed to exchange military physicians who were captives. White seized the opportunity and claimed he was a physician. The Confederates fell for the ruse and exchanged him at Macon, Georgia. From there Harry White proceeded to Pennsylvania where the Republican Party used him as a hero on the campaign trail garnering votes for Lincoln in the 1864 presidential campaign.[40]

As some veterans found their way home to Indiana County, new recruits came forward. In September 1864, the last full contingent of Indiana County recruits organized as the 206th Pennsylvania. Indiana County provided over 650 new soldiers in seven companies of the new regiment. Many of the volunteers had served in the nine-month regiments, the 135th and the 177th, in 1862 and 1863. Among these was Hugh Brady, who had been the lieutenant colonel 177th Pennsylvania, and became the 206th's ranking officer. The 206th joined the Union siege outside Petersburg where the men handled provost duty and served as military laborers in noncombat areas.[41]

After a summer of hard fighting both armies settled around Petersburg, a vital Confederate railway center, south of Richmond. Here Grant's forces entered into a long siege that lasted from September 1864 until the final stages of the war in March 1865. By this time the original enlistees from Indiana County were completing their three-year tour of duty and returning home. Their replacements, either from bounty-induced enlistments or the drafts, lacked the sense of community and local pride that original companies had enjoyed. Now Indiana County soldiers were scattered in various regiments serving in a variety of roles.

John Snyder served as a mail carrier at Petersburg. Ridiculed for having a soft job, John relished the story of his substitute for one day whom rebel sharpshooters tried to pick off as he delivered the mail to Union rifle pits. When he had finished delivering the mail he "informed Snyder he must get well for next trip, as I had very little interest in his job."[42]

William Fair, also from Indiana County, served in the 50th Pennsylvania at Petersburg. His letter in March 1865 described the entrenchments which the Union army had constructed in its siege of Petersburg. The space between the two armies was only fifty rods and "in some places only a stone's throw" apart. "Our line of works," he explained, "is constructed of digging a trench four or five feet deet [sic] timbered in front so as to support an embankment as high as a mans head. This protects the men from the rebs musketry." By this time Fair and other Union soldiers detected the demoralization among the rebels. As many as five hundred Confederates were deserting their army each day and coming over to the Union lines. They "all tell of the same story about suffering in the South." Consequently the Union soldiers were in high spirits and "all think the war will play out this summer."[43]

It was during the Petersburg siege that two of Indiana County's African-American soldiers gained fame. James Bronson, who had enlisted in the 5th United States Colored Troops in Ohio, was first sergeant of Company D. In late September 1864 his regiment participated in one of the key attacks on the Confederate lines. The thrust of the Union strike was on Confederate fortifications, Forts Gilmer, Gregg and Harrison, between Petersburg and Richmond. The initial assaults, generally known as the battle of Chaffin's Farm, occurred on September 29. It was a vicious fight with no significant outcome. Bronson's regiment along with other Union regiments stormed Fort Gilmer in the face of devasting fire. Bronson's company, Company D, lost all of its officers and as the first sergeant he assumed command. His company charged to within one hundred yards of the fort. But it could not withstand the withering fire of the Confederate guns and had to abandon its assault. In the same engagement Alexander Kelly, who was the first sergeant in Company F, 6th United States Colored Troops, grabbed the regimental colors as the color bearer was shot, rallied his men from a state of confusion, and held their position. Like the 5th U.S.C.T., Kelly's regiment could not break the Confederate entrenchments and had to withdraw. For their meritorious roles in leading the attack, Bronson and Kelly received the Congressional Medal of Honor.[44]

The Union siege against the Confederate army at Petersburg continued on through the winter months of 1864–1865. By March 1865 the Confederate army was bleeding with desertions, and morale sagged to its lowest point. Lee, on March 29, ordered an attack in hopes that his army might break out of the siege. But his army was overpowered and the attack collapsed. Grant now became emboldened and ordered a full assault against the Confederate lines. Lee's army could not withstand the Union offensive, surrendered the Petersburg lines, and fled into central Virginia. Lee's retreat left the door wide open for the Union capture of Richmond.[45]

The 206th Pennsylvania which included Indiana Countians was among the first units to enter Richmond. Hugh Brady and his men in the 206th were responsible for maintaining order in one-quarter of Richmond. John Lowry, writing from the anteroom of the Confederate Capitol which the 206th occupied, reported:[46]

> The city presents a deserted appearance. The Aristocracy are retired, and when on the streets pretend to not recognize the soldiers. The colored population is out in great numbers, enjoying a stroll in the Capitol grounds . . . Great destitution prevails.

George W. Stephens offered a similar report. The Union soldiers in the 206th Pennsylvania extinguished fires that threatened magnificent buildings in Richmond but much devastation existed throughout the city.[47]

Back home in Indiana County the people learned of the news of the fall of Richmond just as they had learned of the news of the firing on Fort Sumter. On Monday, April 3, 1864, the noon train, adorned with red, white, and blue bunting, steamed into town. People knew the train bore important news and crowds began to assemble. Upon learning of the fall of Richmond church bells tolled, a general meeting was quickly convened, and state senator St. Clair, Harry White, and Dan Porter gave celebratory speeches. Row, the editor of the *Register*, announced that "BABYLON IS FALLEN."[48]

With the Union army's breakthrough at Petersburg and Lee's retreat, the Confederacy quickly caved in. Grant's army corralled the Confederates at Appomattox Court House and on April 9, 1865, Lee surrendered. A few weeks later, April 18, Joe Johnston, commanding the last Confederate army, capitulated to William T. Sherman in North Carolina, and the American Civil War was over. Editor Row, citing the 118th Psalm, said, "O give thanks unto the Lord."[49]

By May and June the soldiers streamed homeward to anxious wives, parents, and neighbors. Surely, the joyful tears and welcoming hugs for the moment obscured the changes in the soldiers which the war had instilled. Some changes were obvious; R. F. Templeton's mother did not immediately recognize her son who had grown from "a smooth face boy to a bearded man." For others it would take them days and months to assess their experiences and reconcile to a new life. But they would remember the homecoming with fondness and delight. Some thirty years afterward one veteran recalled that when he came home his mother was veiled and trying to swarm a hive of bees. Suddenly she recognized her son and screamed, "Oh, here's Bob!" He remembered, "And I was home again."[50]

Indiana Countians, like people elsewhere, had participated fully in the main currents sweeping through the country. They had fought in every major battle in the East and participated in significant western campaigns. Over four hundred had lost their lives and four Indiana Countians were awarded the Congressional Medal of Honor. A generation later J. T. Stewart compiled a roster of Civil War veterans in the county. While he acknowledged that a few names on the list may have come from neighboring counties, the roster gives 2,831 men who served. This list includes people who were in three-year, one-year, nine-month regiments and special militia.[51] The 1860 census for Indiana County shows that 7,104 males were in the age cohort 15–45, presumably the age group for soldiers. By comparing the Stewart list with the eligible males we can see that approximately 40 percent of the males in Indiana County in 1860 had some military service during the Civil War. Stewart's roster omitted the African-American soldiers from Indiana County. Though the Civil War was about constitutionalism and freedom, Indiana Countians, like most Northerners, were not abolitionists. Hence, during the war and generations afterward, they were oblivious to the status of the African-American.

Still, with the surrender at Appomattox, all Indiana Countians—eager volunteers and reluctant draftees, wives and mothers, farmers and laborers—knew they had engaged in a major chapter in the nation's history. Some had given their lives, others had deferred their dreams, and many, like the widowed Katherine White and the crippled A. J. Bolar, would bear the pain the rest of their lives. Yet, they knew—as we do today—that when the nation was at peril, Indiana Countians had stepped forward to pay whatever price that patriotism demanded.

NOTES

PREFACE

1. Phillip Shaw Paludan's *"A People's Contest": The Union and the Civil War, 1861–1865* (New York: Harper and Row, 1988); Emory Thomas, *The Confederate Nation, 1861–1865* (New York: Harper and Row, 1979); Daniel E. Sutherland, "Getting the 'Real War' Into the Books," *The Virginia Magazine of History and Biography*, 98 (1990), 201.
2. J. Matthew Gallman, *Mastering Wartime: A Social History of Philadelphia During the Civil War* (New York: Cambridge University Press, 1990), is one of the best of the studies in this new genre. Iver Bernstein, *The New York City Draft Riots: Their Significance for American Society and Politics in the Age of the Civil War* (New York: Oxford University Press, 1990), explores the political history of that city. For Chicago, we have two studies—Theodore J. Karamanski, *Rally 'Round the Flag: Chicago and the Civil War* and Robin Einhorn, "The Civil War and Municipal Government in Chicago," in Maris A. Vinovskis, *Toward a Social History of the American Civil War* (New York: Cambridge University Press, 1990). Emily J. Harris, "Sons and Soldiers: Deerfield, Massachusetts and the Civil War," *Civil War History*, 30 (1984), 157–171, is a minor classic in local and Civil War history. For the South, Daniel Sutherland revealed the trauma of citizens in Culpeper County, Virginia as they were caught in the pathway of war. See his "Introduction to War: The Civilians of Culpeper County, Virginia," *Civil War History* 37 (1991), 120–137.

Cultural and intellectual historians have pursued a different, but related, line of inquiry. They have examined the temperament and social values of the American people. Notably, in this category is Anne C. Rose, *Victorian America and the Civil War* (New York: Cambridge University Press, 1992).

CHAPTER 1

1. *The Indiana Progress*, January 6, 1897; the date had to be April 15 for on April 16 the *Indiana Weekly Register* reported the fall of Fort Sumter. The Pennsylvania Railroad station was located at 8th Street, not the surviving one at 11th Street. *The Indiana Progress* printed a series of veterans' memories in 1897.
2. Clarence Stephenson, *Indiana County: 175th Anniversary History* (Indiana: The A. G. Halldin Publishing Company, 1978), I, 147–148, 262, 551–555; U.S.

Manuscript Census, 1860; U.S. Census Bureau, *Agriculture from the 1860 Census*; U.S. Census Bureau, *Manufactures from the 1860 Census*; U.S. Census Bureau, *Compendium of the Ninth Census, 1872*; *Indiana Weekly Register*, December 25, 1860; Peelor's Map, 1856.

3. Eric Foner, *Free Soil, Free Labor, Free Men* (New York: Oxford University Press, 1971).

4. November 6, 1861.

5. Stephenson, *Indiana County*, I, 365–452 details the antislavery movement, and early Republicanism, 589–593; *Indiana Weekly Register*, January 8, 1861.

6. Election returns as reported in the *Indiana Weekly Register*, November 1860; state totals from Arnold Shankman, *The Pennsylvania Antiwar Movement, 1861–1865* (Rutherford, N.J.:Fairleigh Dickinson University Press, 1980).

7. December 4, 1860.

8. James McPherson, *Battle Cry of Freedom* (New York: Oxford University Press, 1988), 248–254.

9. *Indiana Weekly Register*, December 25, 1860.

10. Ibid., January 29, April 23, 1861; U.S. Manuscript Census, 1860.

11. *Indiana Weekly Register*, April 23, 1861.

12. Philip S. Paludan, "The American Civil War Considered as a Crisis in Law and Order," *American Historical Review*, 77 (October 1972), 1013–1034.

13. *Providence Daily Post*, November 19, 1860, quoted in McPherson, *Battle Cry of Freedom*, 247.

14. April 16, 1861.

15. John Pollock to Violet Doty, November 25, 1861, quoted in Clarence Stephenson, *Indiana County*, III, 167.

16. *Indiana Weekly Register*, April 23, 1861.

17. *Indiana Weekly Register*, April 23, 1861; *The Indiana Progress*, January 6, 1897.

18. *Indiana Weekly Register*, April 23, 30, May 7, 14, 1861; *The Indiana Progress*, January 6, 1897.

19. *The Indiana Progress*, February 3, 1897.

20. *Indiana Weekly Register*, May 14, 1861.

21. Robert R. Means, Brookville to Andrew G. Curtin, May 21, 1861; William Cummins, Chambersville to A. G. Curtin, June 13, 1861; Alexander Shoup, Indiana, to General E. M. Biddle, May 20, 1861; W. M. Stewart, Indiana, to Andrew G. Curtin, April 19, 1861; Harry White, Indiana, to A. G. Curtin, May 31, 1861; Thomas White to A. G. Curtin, June 9, 1861, General Correspondence, Office of the Adjutant General, Record Group 19, Pennsylvania Archives. Hereafter cited as OAG, RG.

22. A. J. Bolar (Captain), Armagh, to Governor Curtin, May 5, 18, 1861; W. H. Morgan, Blairsville, to A. G. Curtin, June 5, 1861, OAG, RG 19.

23. E. P. Hildebrand, Indiana, to Eli Slifer, May 9, 1861, Slifer-Dill Collection, Dickinson College; W. M. Stewart et al. to Andrew G. Curtin, May 30, 1861, OAG, RG 19. Stewart and his petitioners had crossed out "five or six."

24. *The Indiana Progress*, December 1, 1897.

25. Thomas White, Indiana, to Andrew G. Curtin, February 20, 1862, Slifer-Dill Collection, Dickinson College; *Indiana Weekly Register*, May 7, 14, June 11, 18, 21, Nov. 5, 1861; Wiley, 133; Henry Wilson Storey, *History of Cambria County, Pennsylvania* (New York: The Lewis Publishing Company), II, 1907, 42–43.

26. Stephenson, *History of Indiana County*, III, 196; *Indiana Weekly Register*, June 25, July 16, July 30, 1861; Thomas White to Major Richard White, May 15, 1861, White Family Papers, University of Virginia.

27. August 6, 20, September 3, 1861.

28. Richard White to Harry White, September 5, 1861, Harry White Papers, Historical Society of Indiana County. Hereafter cited as White MSS. J. T. Gibson,

History of the Seventy-Eighth Pennsylvania Volunteer Infantry (Pittsburgh: The Pittsburgh Printing Co., 1905), 16; *Indiana Weekly Register*, July 23, 1861.

29. Ibid., August 27, 1861; *The Indiana Progress*, February 3, 1897; Christopher T. Arms and E. White, *History of Indiana County, Penna.* (Salem, W.Va.: Walsworth Publishing Company, 1981 reprint), 272.

30. Service Records, National Archives, RG 94; *Indiana Weekly Register*, October 15, 1861; *The Indiana Progress*, December 1, 1897; Arms and White, *History of Indiana County, Penna.*, 280; Kate Scott, *History of the One Hundred and Fifth Regiment of Pennsylvania Volunteers* (Philadelphia: New-World Publishing Company, 1877), 298, 322; Samuel T. Wiley, *Biographical and Historical Cyclopedia of Indiana and Armstrong Counties, Pennsylvania* (Indiana, Pa.: John Graham & Co., 1891), 91.

31. *Indiana Weekly Register*, August 27, September 17, October 8, 1861; *Indiana Messenger*, January 8, 1862; Samuel Carbaugh to brother, August 21, 1861; Carbaugh to parents, November 21, 1861, Pension Records, RG 15, National Archives. For a full biography of Samuel Carbaugh, see Charles Day, "The Efforts and Sacrifices of Samuel Carbaugh," *Westmoreland History*, I (Fall 1995), 16–21.

32. *Indiana Weekly Register*, October 15, December 17, 1861; Andrew J. Bolar Diary (typescript), Helman Collection, Indiana County Historical Society.

33. December 1, 1861; Samuel Carbaugh to parents, November 10, 1861, Pension records, NA.

34. Ibid., November 25, 1861, January 14, 1862; *Indiana Messenger*, January 1, 1862; Bolar Diary; James Hall to Henry Hall, February 9, 1862, Hall Papers.

35. *Indiana Weekly Register*, February 11, 1862; *Indiana Messenger*, January 29, February 5, 12, March 5, 12, 1862.

36. Quoted in McPherson, *Battle Cry of Freedom*, 403.

37. March 19, 1862.

38. Harry White to Thomas White, February 17, 1862, White MSS.

39. R. H. Fair to William Fair, January 21, 1862, Fair Family Papers, Harrisburg Civil War Roundtable Collection, United States Military History Institute (USMHI).

CHAPTER 2

1. *Indiana Progress*, October 6, 1897.

2. Ibid., March 10, 1897.

3. All demographic data comes from the 1860 Manuscript Census; *Indiana Progress*, February 3, 1897.

4. McPherson, *Battle Cry of Freedom*, 606.

5. Craig S. Petrasic, *Who Was the Civil War Soldier?: Enlistment in Indiana County, Pennsylvania*, M.A. thesis, Indiana University of Pennsylvania, 1992, presents a full analysis of Company A, 61st Pennsylvania.

6. Richard A. Sauers, *Advance the Colors* (Harrisburg: Capitol Preservation Committee, 1987), I, 80; Arms & White, *History of Indiana County*, 267; Wiley, *Biographical and Historical Cyclopedia*, 145–147; Douglas R. Cubbison, "That Gallant Company," *Indiana County Heritage* 9 (Summer 1984), 15–19; A. J. Bolar's service and pension records, National Archives.

7. Richard White to Thomas White, April 2, 1862, White MSS.

8. Arms & White, *History of Indiana County*, 270–271.

9. Ibid., 272.

10. Ibid., 295.

11. Gibson, *History of the Seventy-Eighth*, 24–46.

12. Luther S. Dickey, *History of the 103d Regiment, Pennsylvania Veteran Volunteer Regiment* (Chicago: L. S. Dickey, 1910), 91, 382.

13. Wiley, *Biographical and Historical Cyclopedia*, 91; Arms & White, *History of Indiana County*, 280; Scott, *History of the One Hundred and Fifth*, 198, 203–204, 298, 322.

14. *Indiana Progress*, October 20, 1897.

15. Gerald F. Linderman, *Embattled Courage* (New York: The Free Press, 1987), 115.

16. Stephenson, *Indiana County*, III, 166–167.

17. Wesley W. Bell to James Johnston Bell, December 8, 1861, Miscellaneous Civil War Manuscripts, Historical Society of Indiana County.

18. *Indiana Progress*, March 3, 1897.

19. February 9, 1862, Hall MSS.

20. Ibid., April 1, 1862.

21. November 5, December 16, 1861, August 26, 1862, John Uncapher Diary, Historical Society of Blairsville; Arms & White, *History of Indiana County*, 442.

22. Ibid., February 1, 1862.

23. John Park Barbor Diary, USMHI.

24. Ibid.

25. Paddy Griffith, *Battle Tactics of the Civil War* (New Haven: Yale University Press, 1989), 106.

26. Stephenson, *Indiana County*, III, 168–169, 171.

27. McPherson, *Battle Cry of Freedom*, 461.

28. U.S. War Department, *The War of the Rebellion: A Compilation of the Official Records of the Union and Confederate Armies* (Washington: Government Printing Office, 1880–1901), ser. I, vol. 11, pt. 1, 873–875, 896–898. Hereafter cited as *O.R.* A. T. Brewer, *History of the Sixty-First Regiment: Pennsylvania Volunteers, 1861–1865* (Pittsburgh: Art Engraving and Printing Co., 1911), 11–12, 24–25; Samuel Bates, *History of the Pennsylvania Volunteers*, II, 408; Arms & White, *History of Indiana County*, 273, 295; *Indiana Progress*, February 3, 1897.

29. James Hall to Henry Hall, June 10, 1862, Hall MSS; *O.R.*, ser. I, vol. 11, pt. 1, 843, 850–851.

30. *O.R.*, ser. I, vol. 11, pt. 1, 761; William Freeman Fox, *Regimental Losses in the American Civil War, 1861–1865* (Dayton, Ohio: Morningside Bookshop, 1974), 37.

31. *O.R.*, ser. I, vol. 11, pt. 1, 896.

32. Bates, *History of the Pennsylvania Volunteers*, II, 408; Arms & White, *History of Indiana County*, 273, 295; Stephenson, *Indiana County*, III, 171.

33. *O.R.*, ser. I, vol. 11, pt. 1, 850–851.

34. June 27, 1862, Uncapher Diary.

35. *O.R.*, ser. I, vol. 51, pt. 1, 114; *Indiana Weekly Register*, July 29, 1862; *Indiana Progress*, August 18, 1897; Elizabeth Fair Allison to n.p., n.d., Fair Family MSS; Caldwell, *History of Indiana County*, 267; J. R. Sypher, *History of the Pennsylvania Reserve Corps* (Lancaster: Elias Barr & Co., 1865), 262.

36. *Indiana Progress*, January 27, July 28, 1897; *O.R.*, ser. I, vol. 51, pt. 1, 114; Sypher, *History of the Pennsylvania Reserve Corps*, 270–297; Arms & White, *History of Indiana County*, 267; *Indiana Weekly Register*, July 29, 1862. Shambaugh received the Medal of Honor on July 17, 1866; Howard received his on March 30, 1898. U.S. Senate, *Medal of Honor Recipients, 1863–1968*, Washington: Government Printing Office, 1968.

37. James Hall to Henry Hall, July 8, 1862, Hall MSS; Brewer, *History of the Sixty-First Regiment*, 35–36; Scott, *History of the One Hundred and Fifth*, 50.

38. *Indiana Weekly Register*, September 9, 1862.

39. *Indiana Progress*, August 4, 1897.

40. Samuel McCartney Jackson, *Diary of S. M. Jackson for the Year 1862*, (Apollo, Pa.: pref., 1925), 44. Incidentally one should note that General Jackson was the maternal grandfather of Indiana County's famed actor, Jimmy Stewart.

James Maitland Stewart, the paternal grandfather, enlisted in the Signal Corps on January 1, 1864.

41. Diary of Samuel William Campbell, September 6, 1862, Rudolph Haerle Collection, USMHI.
42. *Jackson, Diary of General S. M. Jackson*, 47; *O.R.*, ser. I, vol. 51, pt. 1, 153; *Indiana Progress*, August 11, 18, 1897; Stephen W. Sears, *Landscape Turned Red: The Battle of Antietam* (New Haven: Ticknor & Fields, 1983), 128–149.
43. *O.R.*, ser. I, vol. 51, pt. 1, 154–155.
44. *Indiana Progress*, August 18, 1897.
45. *O.R.*, ser. I, vol. 63, 154–155; Sears, *Landscape Turned Red*, 180–202, 296.
46. *Indiana Weekly Register*, September 30, 1862; *Indiana Progress*, August 18, 1897.
47. McPherson, *Battle Cry of Freedom*, 571–572.
48. Sypher, *History of the Pennsylvania Reserve Corps*, 412–416; McPherson, *Battle Cry of Freedom*, 571–572; Andrew J. Bolar to Congressman J. D. Patten, January 19, 1884, Bolar Pension Records, NA; Samuel Carbaugh to parents, February 16, 1863, Pension Records, NA. The 61st and 105th played the role of reserve units at Fredericksburg.
49. Sypher, *History of the Pennsylvania Reserves*, 433–434.
50. July 8, 1862.
51. September 9, 1862.
52. Compiled from regimental histories, J. T. Stewart, *Indiana County*, and the draft quota.
53. *Indiana Progress*, December 1, 1897.
54. *Indiana Democrat*, October 2, 1862.
55. E. E. Lewis to Harvey Lewis, November 2, 1862, Jacob Frantz Estate, Historical Society of Indiana County.
56. John C. Rugh to Martin Wiley, February 18, 1863, John C. Rugh Papers, owned by Mr. and Mrs. James Wiley.
57. *Indiana Weekly Register*, September 30, 1862.
58. *Indiana Progress*, March 10, 1897.

CHAPTER 3

1. *Indiana Weekly Register*, July 29, 1862.
2. *Indiana Messenger*, August 6, 1862.
3. Allen Nevins, *War for the Union*, II (New York: Charles Scribner's Son, 1960), 163.
4. James W. Geary, *We Need Men: The Union Draft in the Civil War* (Dekalb: Northern Illinois Press, 1991), 28.
5. *Indiana Weekly Register*, July 29, 1862.
6. *Indiana Democrat*, July 31, 1862; *Indiana Weekly Register*, August 19, 26, 1862; Personal Service Record of Hannibal K. Sloan, National Archives.
7. August 5, 1862.
8. Ibid.
9. *Indiana Weekly Register*, August 12, 1862.
10. *Indiana Weekly Register*, August 9, September 9, 1862.
11. *Indiana Weekly Register*, September 2, 1862.
12. Lloyd Jones, Norristown, to Eli Slifer, September 24, 1862, Slifer-Dill Collection, Dickinson College; *Indiana Weekly Register*, September 30, 1862.
13. McPherson, *Battle Cry of Freedom*, 561; Arnold Shankman, *The Pennsylvania Antiwar Movement, 1861–1865*, 101; *Indiana Weekly Register*, November 13, 1860.

14. Report of I. W. Watt, January 19, 1863, Box 2415, Record of Drafted Men, 1862, Office of the Adjutant General, RG 19, Pennsylvania State Archives; *Indiana Weekly Register*, October 21, 30, 1862; Conscientious Objector Depositions, Office of the Adjutant General, Group 19, Pennsylvania State Archives.

15. Geary, *We Need Men*, 65–66.

16. Peter Levine, "Draft Evasion in the North during the Civil War, 1863–1865," *Journal of American History*, 67 (1981), 816–834.

17. McPherson, *Battle Cry of Freedom*, 600–602.

18. Manuscript Census, 1860; Personal Service Record, NA; Bates, *History of the Pennsylvania Volunteers*, II, 131.

19. *Indiana Weekly Register*, May 24, July 1, 1863; Proceedings of the Board of Enrollment, May 1863–Jan. 1865, 21st Congressional District, National Archives, RG 110. All items relating to the draft are from the 21st Congressional District.

20. October 26, 1863, Coulter to PMG James B. Fry, Letters of the Board, NA, RG 110.

21. *Indiana Weekly Register*, July 1, 13, 1863; Proceedings of the Board; June 12, 1865, Historical Report of 21st Military District, (NARA Microfilm M1163, reel #5), NA, RG 110.

22. July 15, 1863, Proceedings of the Board; Coulter to Colonel J. V. Bouford, November 10, 1863, Letters Sent, NA, RG 110.

23. Proceedings of the Board, NA, RG 110; Coulter to Captain C. P. Clark, Inspector for Pennsylvania, November 5, 1863, Letters Sent, NA, RG 110; *Indiana Weekly Register*, August 8, December 9, 1863.

24. G. Sypher, Indiana, to James Hall, June 8, 1863, Hall MSS.

25. *Indiana Weekly Register*, December 9, 1863.

26. *Indiana Weekly Register*, December 23, 1863.

27. *Indiana Weekly Register*, January 13, 1864; Descriptive Books of Enlisted Recruits and Substitutes, Book #15, 23, NA, RG 110.

28. Coulter to Colonel J. V. Bouford, February 20, 1864, Letters of the Board, NA, RG 110.

29. Coulter to Bouford, March 2, 15, 1864, Letters of the Board, NA, RG 110.

30. *Indiana Weekly Register*, March 30, 1864.

31. *Indiana Weekly Register*, April 13, 20, 1864; Descriptive Books of Enlisted Recruits and Substitutes, Books #14 & #15; Service Records of Bronson and Patterson, NA.

32. *Indiana Weekly Register*, April 20, 1864.

33. Continuance Docket, Court of Common Pleas, ICO, 1862–1864, vol. 18, pg. 511; *Speer et al. vs. Blairsville School Directors, Burgess, and Town Council*, Indiana County Court of Common Pleas, microfilm #64.

34. Shankman, *The Pennsylvania Antiwar Movement*, 151–152.

35. *Pennsylvania State Reports*, II, 1866, p. 167.

36. Ibid., 172.

37. Ibid., 179.

38. Ibid., 170.

39. Ibid., 172.

40. Ibid., 157.

41. Ibid., 160.

42. Ibid., 163.

43. Ibid., 164.

44. Ibid., 164.

45. Ibid., 165.

46. Descriptive Books of Enlisted Recruits and Substitutes, Book #15, 24, NA, RG 110; Historical Report, NA, RG 110; *Indiana Democrat*, June 16, 23, 1864.

47. Coulter to PMG James B. Fry, August 21, 1864; Coulter to Captain R. J. Dodge, AAPMG, Harrisburg, August 31, 1864, Letters of the Board, NA, RG 110; Historical Report, NA, RG 110.

48. *Indiana Weekly Register,* August 31, 1863.
49. February 8, 1865.
50. February 16, 1865.
51. Coulter to Fry, March 31, 1865, Letters of the Board, NA, RG 110; *Indiana Weekly Register,* February 8, 1865.
52. Coulter to Captain R. J. Dodge, AAPMG, Harrisburg, February 28, 1865, Letters of the Board, NA, RG 110; *Indiana Democrat,* February 16, 1865; *O.R.,* ser. III, vol. 4, 744–745.
53. McPherson, *Battle Cry of Freedom,* 607.
54. October 13, 1865, Office of the Provost Marshal, 22nd District, Pittsburgh to AAPMG, Harrisburg. Though emanating from the 22nd District, this letter totals the 21st District bounties, too. Letters Received, 21st District, NA, RG 110.
55. Coulter to Dodge, February 3, 1865, Letters of the Board, NA, RG 110.
56. A. A. Barker, Ebensburg, to PM Coulter, Febuary 10, 1865; Jacob Kirkpatrick et al. to Board of Enrollment of Indiana County, March 1, 1865, Letters Received, NA, RG 110.
57. Historical Report, NA, RG 110.

CHAPTER 4

1. *Indiana Weekly Register,* February 24, 1863.
2. Bronson presents a puzzle for the local historian. Various spellings of the name, e.g., Bronson, Brunson, and Brunston, and different middle initials, G and H, and several James's cause problems in precise identification. U.S. Manuscript Census, Indiana County, 1860; James H. Bronson Personal Service Record, NA; Frank Levstik, "The Fifth Regiment, United States Colored Troops, 1863–1865," *Northwest Ohio Quarterly,* 42 (1970), 86–98. For Kelly, the best source is Wes Slusher and Joe Pulgini, *Allegheny County Medal of Honor Recipients* (Pittsburgh: Allegheny County Board of Commissioners, 1991).
3. Marlin L. Bracken to brother, June 17, 1863, Martin L. Bracken Letters, Soldiers and Sailors Memorial Hall, Pittsburgh; Bates, *History of the Pennsylvania Volunteers,* IV, 1253–1254.
4. John McNutt to J. M. Wiley, January 12, 31, 1863, John McNutt Letters, owned by Mr. and Mrs. James Wiley.
5. Findley Carney told this story on his 101st birthday. Roy Decker shared a newspaper clipping from 1938 that told this story.
6. *Indiana Democrat,* March 12, 1863; J. T. Gibson, *History of the Seventy-Eighth Pennsylvania* (Pittsburgh: The Pittsburgh Printing Co., 1905), 47–64, 178–184; McPherson, *Battle Cry of Freedom,* 580–582; James Lee McDonough, *Stones River: Bloody Winter in Tennessee* (Knoxville: The University of Tennessee Press, 1980), 109–150, 200–201; *Battles and Leaders* (New York: Thomas Yoseloff, Inc., 1956), III, 619–622.
7. Harry White to A. Mullin, February 26, 1863; W. M. Stewart to Governor Curtin, March 23, 1863; James P. Speer to Governor Curtin, March 7, 1863. Correspondence Folder, 40th Regiment, Records of the Department of Military Affairs, Office of the Adjutant General, Reel 43, RG 19; Service Records of James Porter and Hannibal Sloan, NA.
8. Edward J. Stackpole, *Chancellorsville: Lee's Greatest Battle* (Harrisburg: Stackpole Co., 1958), 238–247.
9. Arms & White, *A History of Indiana County,* 281; Bates, *History of the Pennsylvania Volunteers,* III, 784; Scott, *History of the One Hundred and Fifth Regiment,* 72–77, 203–205.
10. Stackpole, *Chancellorsville: Lee's Greatest Battle,* 243.
11. *Indiana Progress,* June 30, 1897; Brewer, *History of the Sixty-First Regiment,* 53–57; *O.R.* ser. I, vol. 51, pt. 1, 185–186.

12. Bates, *History of the Pennsylvania Volunteers*, III, 577–578; Muffly, *The Story of Our Regiment*, 83–84, 88, 631–632, 657, 970.
13. Bates, *History of the Pennsylvania Volunteers*, III, 302–303; John Parke Barbor Diary, May 4, 5, 1863, USMHI.
14. John Parke Barbor Diary, May 27, 1863, February 14, 1864; Robert F. Templeton to Mrs. E. H. Martin, August 13, 1863, Robert Templeton Letters, Historical Society of Indiana County; Mary Hall, Indiana, to James Hall, August 21, 1863, Hall MSS.
15. Edwin Coddington, *The Gettysburg Campaign: A Study in Command* (New York: Charles Scribner's Sons, 1968) 137, 144–152.
16. *Indiana Weekly Register*, July 1, 8, 1863.
17. Campbell Diary, Rudolph Haerle Collection, Military History Institute; Arms & White, *History of Indiana County*, 399.
18. Stewart, *Indiana County*, I, 580–588; Harry White to Thomas White, January 8, June 3, 9, August 5, October 11, November 15, 1862, White MSS.
19. Harry White to Thomas White, May 26, June 12, 1863, White MSS.
20. Wilbur Sturtevant Nye, *Here Come the Rebels!* (Baton Rouge: Louisiana State University Press, 1965), 39, 66–67, 86–89; O.R., 27, pt. 2, 86–87.
21. Nye, *Here Come the Rebels!*, 108–110.
22. Nye, *Here Come the Rebels!*, 119–120; O.R., 27, pt. 2, 151; *Indiana Progress*, March 3, May 12, 1897.
23. Coddington, *The Gettysburg Campaign: A Study in Command*, 268–271; O.R. ser. I, vol. 27, pt. 1, 288; Stewart, *Indiana County*, I, 154–156.
24. McPherson, *Battle Cry of Freedom*, 656–657.
25. Matthias Manner Diary, privately owned by Clarence Stephenson, quoted in Harry W. Pfanz, *Gettysburg: The Second Day* (Chapel Hill: The University of North Carolina Press, 1987) 303; O.R. ser. I, vol. 27, pt. 1, 500; *Indiana Progress*, October 27, 1897.
26. O.R., ser. I, vol. 27, pt. 1, 177, 500–501; Pfanz, *Gettysburg: The Second Day*, 330–333; Bates, *The Pennsylvania Volunteers*, 785.
27. J. W. Muffly, *The Story of Our Regiment*, 536; Pfanz, *Gettysburg: The Second Day*, 285–286.
28. Sypher, *The Pennsylvania Reserves*, 448; *Pennsylvania at Gettysburg* (Harrisburg: E. K. Meyers, State Printer, 1893), 260–261.
29. Sypher, *The Pennsylvania Reserves*, 441; *Pennsylvania at Gettysburg*, I, 259, 262–263; Pfanz, *Gettysburg: The Second Day*, 396–399.
30. Pfanz, *Gettysburg: The Second Day*, 402.
31. Brewer, *History of the Sixty-First Regiment*, 62–64. After the battle of Gettysburg Creps was admitted to a hospital where he recovered. The inflammation returned in 1864 and pestered him the remainder of his life. Pension Records, NA.
32. Muffly, *The Story of Our Regiment*, 880–881.
33. William Penn Oberlin to Annie Oberlin, July 10, 1863, William Penn Oberlin Papers, Historical Society of Indiana County.
34. Manner Diary.
35. McPherson, *Battle Cry of Freedom*, 666–674; Gibson, *History of the Seventy-Eighth Pennsylvania*, 83, 113.
36. Gibson, *History of the Seventy-Eighth Pennsylvania*, 125.

CHAPTER 5

1. *Indiana Democrat*, May 7, 1862.
2. Stephenson, *History of Indiana County*, IV, 83–84.
3. Ibid., 328–329.
4. May 14, 1862.

5. May 14, June 6, June 19, July 3, 1862, January 15, 1863; *Indiana Weekly Register*, January 17, 1863.
6. *Indiana Weekly Register*, June 2, 1863.
7. *The Messenger*, July 30, 1862.
8. George Row to John Covode, August 30, 1854, John Covode Papers, Library of Congress; W. M. Stewart & A. W. Taylor, Indiana, to Joseph Casey, November 27, 1861, Simon Cameron Papers, Library of Congress; Wiley, *Biographical and Historical Cyclopedia*, 155–156.
9. Stewart, *Indiana County*, I, 580–588.
10. Harry White to Thomas White, May 27, June 3, October 11, 1862, White Papers, Historical Society of Indiana County.
11. *Indiana Weekly Register*, October 21, 1862; Shankman, *The Pennsylvania Antiwar Movement*, 101.
12. C. P. Menkle to John Covode, June 24, July 9, 1862, Covode MSS, Library of Congress. Election results taken from *Indiana Weekly Register*, November 13, 1860, October 21, 1862.
13. *Indiana Democrat*, January 15, May 7, June 18, September 10, 1863.
14. Shankman, *The Pennsylvania Antiwar Movement*, 134–136; *Indiana Weekly Register*, October 21, 1863.
15. John P. Penny, "The Critical Period in Pennsylvania History," *Western Pennsylvania Historical Magazine*, 5 (1922), 236–243.
16. Arnold Shankman,"John P. Penney, Harry White, and the 1864 Pennsylvania Senate Deadlock," *Western Pennsylvania Historical Magazine*, 55 (1972), 77; George M. Getty to Thomas White, January 6, 1864, White MSS.
17. *Daily Telegraph* (Harrisburg), February 1, 2, 1864; *Indiana Weekly Register*, February 3, 24, 1864.
18. *Indiana Weekly Register*, November 4, 30, 1864.
19. *Indiana Democrat*, November 13, 1862; Ralph Andreano, ed., *The Economic Impact of the American Civil War* (Cambridge, Mass., 1962), 178, 181.
20. Philip Shaw Paludin, *"A People's Contest": The Union and the Civil War, 1861–1865* (New York: Harper and Row, 1988), 151–169; Bureau of the Census, *Agriculture of the United States*; *Compendium of the Ninth Census*.
21. *Indiana Weekly Register*, February 11, 1862.
22. Stephenson, *History of Indiana County*, I, 193; *Indiana Democrat*, April 24, 1864; *Compendium of the Ninth Census*, 786.
23. Harry N. Scheiber, "Economic Change in the Civil War Era: An Analysis of Recent Studies," *Civil War History*, 11 (1965), 396–411; J. Matthew Gallman, *Mastering Wartime*, 252–253; Bureau of the Census, *Manufactures of the Eighth Census*, 510–511; *Compendium of the Ninth Census*, 725.
24. February 5, 1863.
25. Anne Firor Scott, "On Seeing and Not Seeing: The Case of Historical Invisibility," *Journal of American History*, 71 (June 1984), 7–21.
26. Richard White to Thomas White, June 17, 1862, White MSS; William Penn Oberlin to Annie Oberlin, April 17, 1863, April 10, 1864; John Compton to wife, April 8, 1865, John Compton Papers, owned by Mrs. Thomas S. Barbor; Historical Report, NARA M1163, reel #5, RG 110.
27. George R. Walker Pension Records; Carbaugh Pension Records, National Archives; Sidney Marlin to John Marlin, June 2, 1862, John Marlin Letters, owned by Ellen Blazavich.
28. *Indiana Democrat*, February 5, 1863; *Indiana Weekly Register*, February 3, 1864.
29. John Compton to wife, March 20, 1865, Compton MSS; Sarah Ann Marlin to John Marlin, April 4, 1862, Marlin MSS; Catherine Fair to William Fair, April 16, 30, 1865, Fair Family Papers, Harrisburg Civil War Round Table, USMHI.
30. Sara Ann Marlin to John Marlin, November 26, 1863, Marlin MSS; Catherine Fair to William Fair, April 30, 1865, Fair MSS, MHI.

31. Maris A. Vinovskis, *Toward a Social History of the American Civil War* (New York: Cambridge University Press, 1990), 26–27; *Historical Statistics of U.S.*, I, 165.

32. U.S. Pension Bureau, *List of Pensioners on the Roll, January 1, 1883,* 656–661, *Senate Executive Document* 84, pts. 1–5, 47th Congress, 2nd Session; Day, "The Efforts and Sacrifices of Samuel Carbaugh," *Westmoreland History,* 21.

33. Vinovskis, *Toward A Social History of the American Civil War,* 4–7; see also, Drew Gilpin Faust, *"A Riddle of Death": Mortality and Meaning in the American Civil War,* 34th Annual Robert Fortenbaugh Memorial Lecture, Gettysburg College, 1995.

34. *World War II Honor List of Dead and Missing: State of Pennsylvania,* War Department, 1946; *Personnel Who Died from Hostile Action (Including Missing and Capture) in the Korean War, 1950–1957: Pennsylvania,* Korean Conflict Casualty File, 1950–1957, Records of the Office of the Secretary of Defense, RG 330, NA; *Personnel Who Died (Including Missing and Captured Dead) in the Vietnam War, 1957–1986: Pennsylvania,* Records of the Office of the Secretary of Defense, RG 330, NA; U.S. Department of Commerce, *City and County Data Book,* Washington: Government Printing Office, 1949, 1952, 1962.

35. Eric T. Dean, Jr., "'We Will All be Lost and Destroyed': Post-Traumatic Stress Disorder and the Civil War," *Civil War History,* 37 (1991), 138–153; *Indiana Progress,* January 20, 1897; 1860 Manuscript Census, Indiana County, II, 330; Muster Rolls of the 40th Pennsylvania, (microfilm) State Archives.

CHAPTER 6

1. Harry White Diary, White MSS.

2. Bates, *History of the Pennsylvania Volunteers,* II, 178; *Indiana Weekly Register,* May 17, 1864.

3. Bruce Catton, *A Stillness At Appomattox* (Garden City: Doubleday & Company, 1954), 55–92.

4. *Indiana Progress,* January 27, 1897; Sypher, *The Pennsylvania Reserves,* 511–512; Robert Garth Scott, *Into the Wilderness With the Army of the Potomac* (Bloomington: Indiana University Press, 1985), 37–40.

5. *Indiana Weekly Register,* January 6, 1864; Brewer, *History of the Sixty-First Regiment,* 169.

6. *Indiana Progress,* June 30, 1897.

7. *Indiana Progress,* June 30, 1897; Brewer, *History of the Sixty-First Regiment,* 82–83.

8. Brewer, *History of the Sixty-First Regiment,* 164, 169.

9. Scott, *History of the One Hundred and Fifth,* 94.

10. Ibid., 95.

11. Fox, *Regimental Losses,* 290.

12. Scott, *Into the Wilderness,* 62; Bates, *History of the Pennsylvania Volunteers,* II, 221–222.

13. *Indiana Progress,* May 19, 1897; see also Catton, *A Stillness At Appomattox,* 101.

14. *Indiana Weekly Register,* May 18, 25, 1864.

15. Brewer, *History of the Sixty-First Regiment,* 89.

16. *Indiana Progress,* June 3, 1897.

17. Walker Pension Records, NA.

18. Catton, *A Stillness At Appomattox,* 126.

19. *Indiana Progress,* March 10, 1897.

20. *Indiana Progress,* June 30, 1897.

21. Brewer, *History of the Sixty-First Regiment,* 93–95.

22. Fox, *Regimental Losses,* 274.

23. *Indiana Progress,* June 30, 1897.

24. Newspaper clipping, Fair Family Papers, MHI.
25. Scott, *History of the One Hundred and Fifth*, 100–105, 118–119; Fox, *Regimental Losses*, 290.
26. Fox, *Regimental Losses*, 302; Muffly, *The Story of Our Regiment*, 970–980; William D. Matter, *If It Takes All Summer: The Battle of Spotsylvania* (Chapel Hill: The University of North Carolina Press, 1988), 145–146.
27. Matter, *If It Takes All Summer*, 197.
28. Sypher, *History of the Pennsylvania Reserves*, 545–547.
29. *Indiana Democrat*, June 16, 1864.
30. *Indiana Democrat*, June 16, 1864; Fox, *Regimental Losses*, 256–261.
31. *Indiana Democrat*, June 23, 1864.
32. Brewer, *History of the Sixty-First Regiment*, 103.
33. Ibid., 108–109.
34. Ibid., 114, 148; *Indiana Weekly Register*, September 14, 1864.
35. Gibson, *History of the Seventy-Eighth Pennsylvania*, 196–290.
36. Bates, *History of the Pennsylvania Volunteers*, I, 858; *Indiana Progress*, January 20, April 7, 1897.
37. Dickey, *History of the 103d Regiment*, 59–64, 382.
38. *Indiana Progress*, May 26, 1897.
39. White Pension Records, NA.
40. Harry White to Titian J. Coffey, June 28, 1864; Major W. R. Sterling, Washington, to Thomas White, n.d., August 1864, White MSS; Stewart, *Indiana County*, I, 583–584.
41. Bates, *History of the Pennsylvania Volunteers*, V, 655–670.
42. *Indiana Progress*, February 17, 1897.
43. William Fair to Friend, March 11, 1865, Fair Family Papers, MHI.
44. Richard J. Sommers, *Richmond Redeemed* (Garden City: Doubleday & Company, 1981), 85–88; *Official Roster of the Soldiers of the State of Ohio in the War of the Rebellion, 1861–1866*, 603; U.S. Government, *Medal of Honor Recipients, 1863–1963*, 387; Slusher and Pulgini, *Allegheny County Medal of Honor Recipients*, 8, 13. Apparently, Bronson had wearied of command responsibilities because in November 1864, he requested a reduction in rank to join the regimental brass band. Bronson Service Record, NA.
45. McPherson, *Battle Cry of Freedom*, 844–846.
46. *Indiana Weekly Register*, April 12, 1865.
47. G. W. Stephens to Jenny, April 6, 1864, Stephens MSS.
48. Sister Ellen to William Fair, April 6, 1865, Fair MSS; *Indiana Democrat*, April 6, 1865; *Indiana Weekly Register*, April 5, 1865.
49. *Indiana Weekly Register*, April 12, 1865.
50. *Indiana Progress*, March 3, 1897.
51. Stewart, *Indiana County*, I, 144–176.

BIBLIOGRAPHY

MANUSCRIPTS

John Park Barbour Diary, United States Military History Institute, Carlisle, Pa.

Andrew Bolar Diary (typescript), Historical and Genealogical Society of Indiana County.

Martin L. Bracken Letters, Soldiers and Sailors Memorial Hall, Pittsburgh, Pa.

Simon Cameron Papers, Library of Congress.

Samuel William Campbell Papers, Rudolph Haerle Collection, United States Military History Institute, Carlisle, Pa.

John Compton Papers, owned by Mrs. Thomas S. Barbor.

John Covode Papers, Library of Congress.

Fair Family Papers, Harrisburg Civil War Roundtable, United States Military History Institute, Carlisle, Pa.

Jacob Frantz Estate, Historical and Genealogical Society of Indiana County.

Hall Family Papers, owned Mr. and Mrs. David Russell.

Matthias Manner Diary, owned by Clarence Stephenson.

John Marlin Letters, owned by Ellen Blazavich.

Miscellaneous Civil War Manuscripts, Historical and Genealogical Society of Indiana County.

John McNutt Letters, owned by Mr. & Mrs. James Wiley.

William Penn Oberlin Papers, Historical and Genealogical Society of Indiana County.

114

John C. Rugh Papers, owned by Mr. & Mrs. James Wiley.

Slifer-Dill Collection, Dickinson College.

Stephens Family Papers, owned by Mr. & Mrs. David Russell.

Robert Templeton Letters, Historical and Genealogical Society of Indiana County.

John Uncapher Diary, Historical Society of Blairsville, Indiana County.

Harry White Papers, Historical and Genealogical Society of Indiana County.

White Family Papers, University of Virginia.

NEWSPAPERS

Daily Telegraph (Harrisburg), 1864.

Indiana Democrat, 1862–1865.

Indiana Messenger, 1862–1865.

The Indiana Progress, 1897.

Indiana Weekly Register, 1861–1865.

ARCHIVES

Indiana County, Continuance Docket, Court of Common Pleas, 1862–1864, Volume 18.

———. *Speer et al. vs. Blairsville School Directors, Burgess, and Town Council.* Court of Common Pleas (microfilm, #64).

Pennsylvania. Supreme Court. *Pennsylvania State Reports, 1866.* St. Paul: West Publishing Company, 1866.

Office of the Adjutant General, Conscientious Objector Despositions, RG 19, Pennsylvania State Archives.

———. General Correspondence, RG 19, Pennsylvania State Archives.

———. Records of the Department of Military Affairs, 40th Regiment, RG 19, Pennsylvania State Archives.

———. Records of Drafted Men, 1862, RG 19, Pennsylvania State Archives.

U.S. Bureau of the Census. Manuscript Census, 1860 (microfilm).

———. *Agriculture of the United States of the Eighth Census.* Government Printing Office, 1865.

———. *Compendium of the Ninth Census.* Government Printing Office, 1872.

———. *Manufactures of the United States of the Eighth Census.* Government Printing Office, 1865.

———. *Population of the United States of the Eighth Census.* Government Printing Office, 1865.

U.S. Department of Commerce. *City and County Data Book.* Washington: Government Printing Office, 1949, 1952, 1962.

U.S. Pension Bureau. *List of Pensioners on the Roll, January 1883.* Senate Executive Document 84, Pts. 1–5, 47th Congress, 2nd Session.

U.S. Secretary of Defense. *Personnel Who Died from Hostile Action (Including Missing and Capture) in the Korean War, 1950–1957: Pennsylvania.* Korean Conflict Casualty File, 1950–1957. National Archives, RG 330.

———. *Personnel Who Died (Including Missing and Captured Dead) in the Vietnam War, 1957–1986: Pennsylvania.* National Archives, RG 330.

U.S. Senate. Committee on Labor and Public Welfare. *Medal of Honor Recipients, 1863–1963.* Washington: Government Printing Office, 1968.

U.S. War Department. *The War of the Rebellion: A Compilation of the Official Records of the Union and Confederate Armies.* Washington: Government Printing Office, 1880–1901.

———. Descriptive Books of Enlisted Recruits and Substitutes, Book #15. 21st District, National Archives, RG 110.

———. Historical Report of the 21st Military District, 21st District, National Archives, RG 110.

———. Letters of the Board of Enrollment, 21st District, National Archives, RG 110.

———. Proceedings of the Board of Enrollment, May 1863–January 1865, 21st District, National Archives, RG 110.

———. Office of the Provost Marshal, 22nd District, National Archives, RG 110.

———. Pension Records, National Archives, RG 15.

———. Service Records, National Archives, RG 94.

———. *World War II Honor List of Dead and Missing: State of Pennsylvania,* 1946.

BOOKS

Andreano, Ralph, ed. *The Economic Impact of the American Civil War.* Cambridge, Mass.: Havard University Press, 1962.

Arms, Christopher T., and E. White. *History of Indiana County, Penna.* 1880. Reprint. Salem, W.Va.: Walsworth Publishing Company, 1981.

Bates, Samuel P. *History of the Pennsylvania Volunteers, 1861–65.* Harrisburg: B. Singerly, State Printer, 1869–71. 5 vols.

Battles and Leaders of the Civil War. 4 Vols. New York: Thomas Yoseloff, Inc., 1956.

Bernstein, Iver. *The New York City Draft Riots: Their Significance for American Society and Politics in the Age of the Civil War.* New York: Oxford University Press, 1990.

Brewer, A. T. *History of the Sixty-First Regiment: Pennsylvania Vounteers, 1861–1865.* Pittsburgh: Art Engraving & Printing Co., 1911.

Catton, Bruce. *A Stillness At Appomattox.* Garden City: Doubleday & Company, 1954.

Coddington, Edwin B. *The Gettysburg Campaign: A Study in Command.* New York: Charles Scribner's Sons, 1968.

Dickey, Luther S. *History of the 103d Regiment, Pennsylvania Veteran Volunter Regiment.* Chicago: L. S. Dickey, 1910.

Foner, Eric. *Free Soil, Free Labor, Free Men.* New York: Oxford University Press, 1971.

Fox, William Freeman. *Regimental Losses in the American Civil War, 1861–1865.* Dayton, Ohio: Morningside Bookshop, 1974.

Gallman, J. Matthew. *Mastering Wartime: A Social History of Philadelphia During the Civil War.* New York: Cambridge University Press, 1990.

Geary, James W. *We Need Men: The Union Draft in the Civil War.* Dekalb, Illinois: Northern Illinois University Press, 1991.

Gibson, J. T. *History of the Seventy-Eighth Pennsylvania.* Pittsburgh: The Pittsburgh Printing Co., 1905.

Griffith, Paddy. *Battle Tactics of the Civil War.* New Haven: Yale University Press, 1989.

Jackson, Samuel McCartney. *Diary of General S. M. Jackson for the Year 1862.* Apollo, Pa., pref., 1925.

Linderman, Gerald F. *Embattled Courage.* New York: The Free Press, 1987.

Matter, William D. *If It Takes All Summer: The Battle of Spotsylvania.* Chapel Hill: The University of North Carolina Press, 1988.

McDonough, James Lee. *Stones River: Bloody Winter in Tennessee.* Knoxville: The University of Tennessee Press, 1980.

McPherson, James. *Battle Cry of Freedom.* New York: Oxford University Press, 1988.

Muffly, J. W. *The Story of Our Regiment: A History of the 148th Pennsylvania.* Des Moines, Iowa: The Kenyon Printing & Mfg. Co., 1904.

Nevins, Allen. *The War for the Union.* New York: Charles Scribner's Son, 1960. 2 vols.

Nye, Wibur Sturtevant. *Here Come the Rebels!* Baton Rouge: Louisiana State University Press, 1965.

———. *Official Roster of the Soldiers of the State of Ohio in the War of the Rebellion, 1861–1865.* Akron: The Werner Company, 1893.

Paludan, Philip Shaw. *"A People's Contest": The Union and the Civil War, 1861–1865.* New York: Harper and Row, 1988.

———. *Pennsylvania at Gettysburg.* Harrisburg, E. K. Meyers, State Printer, 1893, 2 vols.

Pfanz, Harry W. *Gettysburg: The Second Day.* Chapel Hill: The University of North Carolina Press, 1987.

Rose, Anne C. *Victorian America and the Civil War.* New York: Cambridge University Press, 1992.

Sauers, Richard A. *Advance the Colors.* Harrisburg: Capitol Preservation Committee, 1987–1991. 2 vols.

Scott, Kate M. *History of the One Hundred and Fifth Regiment of Pennsylvania Volunteers.* Philadelphia: New-World Publishing Company, 1877.

Scott, Robert Garth. *Into the Wilderness With the Army of the Potomac.* Bloomington:Indiana University Press, 1985.

Sears, Stephen W. *Landscape Turned Red: The Battle of Antietam.* New Haven: Ticknor & Fields, 1983.

Shankman, Arnold M. *The Pennsylvania Antiwar Movement, 1861–1865.* Rutherford, N.J.: Fairleigh Dickinson University Press, 1980.

Slusher, Wes, and Joe Pulgini. *Allegheny County Medal of Honor Recipients.* Pittsburgh: Allegheny County Board of Commissioners, 1991.

Sommers, Richard. *Richmond Redeemed.* Garden City: Doubleday & Company, 1981.

Stackpole, Edward J. *Chancellorsville: Lee's Greatest Battle.* Harrisburg: Stackpole Co., 1958.

Stephenson, Clarence D. *Indiana County, 175th Anniversary History.* Indiana, Pa.: The A. G. Halldin Publishing Company, 1978, 4 vols.

Stewart, Joshua Thompson. *Indiana County, Pennsylvania: Her People, Past and Present.* Chicago: J. H. Beers & Co., 1918.

Storey, Henry Wilson. *History of Cambria County, Pennsylvania.* New York: The Lewis Publishing Company, 1907.

Sypher, J. R. *History of the Pennsylvania Reserve Corps.* Lancaster: Elias Barr & Co., 1865.

Thomas, Emory. *The Confederate Nation, 1861–1856.* New York: Harper and Row, 1979.

Vinovskis, Maris A., ed. *Towards a Social History of the American Civil War.* New York: Cambridge University Press, 1990.

Wiley, Samuel T. *Biographical and Historical Cyclopedia of Indiana and Armstrong Counties, Pennsylvania.* Indiana, Pa.: John Gresham & Co., 1891.

ARTICLES

Cubbison, Douglas R. "That Gallant Company," *Indiana County Heritage* 9 (Summer 1984), 15–19.

Day, Charles. "The Efforts and Sacrifices of Samuel Carbaugh," *Westmoreland History* I (Fall 1995), 16–21.

Dean, Eric T. "'We Will All be Lost and Destroyed': Post-Traumatic Stress Disorder and the Civil War," *Civil War History* 37 (1991), 138–153.

Harris, Emily. "Sons and Soldiers: Deerfield, Massachusetts and the Civil War," *Civil War History* 30 (1984), 157–171.

Levine, Peter. "Draft Evasion in the North during the Civil War, 1863–1865," *Journal of American History* 67 (1981), 816–834.

Levstik, Frank. "The Fifth Regiment, United States Colored Troops, 1863–1865," *Northwest Ohio Quarterly* 42 (1970), 86–98.

Paludan, Philip S. The American Civil War Considered as a Crisis in Law and Order," *The American Historical Review* 77 (1972), 1013–1034.

Penny, John C. "The Critical Period in Pennsylvania History," *Western Pennsylvania Historical Magazine* 5 (1922), 236–243.

Scheiber, Harry N. "Economic Change in the Civil War Era: An Analysis of Recent Studies," *Civil War History* 11 (1965), 396–411.

Scott, Anne Firor. "On Seeing and Not Seeing: The Case of Historical Invisibility," *Journal of American History* 71 (1984), 7–21.

Shankman, Arnold. "John P. Penney, Harry White, and the 1864 Pennsylvania Senate Deadlock," *Western Pennsylvania Historical Magazine* 55 (1972), 76–86.

Sutherland, Daniel E. "Getting the 'Real War' Into the Books," *Virginia Magazine of History and Biography* 98 (1990), 193–220.

———. "Introduction to War: The Civilians of Culpeper County, Virginia," *Civil War History* 37 (1991), 120–137.

M.A. THESIS

Petrasic, Craig S. "Who was the Civil War Soldier?: Enlistment in Indiana County, Pennsylvania." Master's thesis, Indiana University of Pennsylvania, 1992.

INDEX